IN THE
RUSSIAN
STYLE

IN THE RUSSIAN

Introduction by **Audrey Kennett** · Designed by **Bryan Holm**

STYLE

Edited by JACQUELINE ONASSIS

With the Cooperation of The Metropolitan Museum of Art

MJF BOOKS
NEW YORK

Winter travel in Russia. Baron von Herberstein, 1557.

Published by MJF Books
Fine Communications
Two Lincoln Square
60 West 66th Street
New York, NY 10023

Library of Congress Catalog Card Number 97-75626
ISBN 1-56731-256-X

10 9 8 7 6 5 4 3 2 1

The Editor wishes to express grateful acknowledgment to the following:
American Heritage Publishing Co. Inc.: for excerpts from *The Horizon Book of the Arts of Russia*, New York, 1970. Audrey and Victor Kennett, Thames and Hudson, London, and G. B. Putnam's Sons, New York: for excerpts from *The Palaces of Leningrad*. Phyllis Penn Kohler: for excerpts from *Custine's Eternal Russia*, Center for Advanced International Studies, University of Miami. Vladimir Nabokov, Princeton University Press, and Routledge & Kegan Paul: for excerpts from *Eugene Onegin* by Alexander Pushkin, translated by Vladimir Nabokov (Bollingen Series LXXII), second edition, © 1975 by Princeton University Press. Oxford University Press, London: for excerpts from *War and Peace* by Leo Tolstoy, translated by Louise and Aylmer Maude. The New American Library, New York; G. P. Putnam's Sons, New York; and McDonald and Jane's, London: for excerpts from *Elizabeth and Catherine, Empresses of all the Russias* by Robert Coughlan.

CONTENTS

ACKNOWLEDGMENTS

The help of many individuals has been important to the completion of this book. Among them, the editor wishes to thank the following:

In the United States

Dr. Leonid Tarassuk
Paul Schaeffer, A La Vieille Russie
Andreas Brown, The Gotham Book Mart
Suzanne Massie

The Metropolitan Museum of Art

Diana Vreeland, Special Consultant to the
Costume Institute
Thomas Hoving, Director
Philip de Montebello, Vice-Director for
Curatorial and Educational Affairs
Karl Katz, Chairman for Special Exhibitions
Jean Mailey, Curator, Textile Study Room
Dr. Helmut Nickel, Curator, Arms and Armor
Margaret Nolan, Chief Librarian
Marica Vilcek, Associate Curator
Mimi Harris, Research Associate,
European Paintings
Vera Ostoia, Curator Emeritus,
The Medieval Department
William Pons, Manager, Photographic Studio
Ferle Bramson, Administrative Assistant
to Mrs. Vreeland
Candace Fischer, Assistant to Mrs. Vreeland

The Viking Press

Gael Towey Dillon	Edwin Kennebeck
Christopher Holme	Lewis P. Lewis
Jay Holme	Delfina Rattazzi
Carol Sue Judy	Olga Zaferatos

In the Soviet Union

Ministry of Culture, Moscow

Pyotr Demichev, Minister of Culture
Vladimir Popov, Deputy Minister of Culture
Anatoly Duyzev, Head, International
Relations Department
Alexander Halturin, Head, Arts Department
Alla Butrova, Western European and
American Department

Cultural Board, Leningrad

Boris M. Skvortsov, Chairman
Anatoly I. Petrunin, Vice Chairman

The State Historical Museum, Moscow

Luisa Efimova, Chief of the Fabric Department

The Kremlin, Moscow

N. G. Nemirov, Director
Nataliya A. Mayasova, Assistant Director

The State Tretyakov Gallery, Moscow

P. I. Lebedev, Director
Vitaly S. Manin, Deputy Director
Anjelika K. Molchanova, Chief Curator

The State Pushkin Museum of Fine Arts, Moscow

Irina A. Antonova, Director

Ostankino, Moscow

Elsa A. Kotlyarova, Director
Ludmila A. Butugina, Chief Curator
Irina L. Petukhova, Curator

The State Hermitage Museum, Leningrad

Dr. Boris Piotrovsky, Director
Vitaly Suslov, Deputy Director for Research
Arcady Poliakov, Deputy Director,
International Department
Tamara Kovshunova, Curator of Russian Costume

The State Russian Museum, Leningrad

Vassily A. Pushkarev, Director

Pavlosk

Valeriya A. Belanina
Anatoly M. Kutchumov

Pushkin — Tsarskoe Selo

Georgy E. Belyaev

Oranienbaum

Ludmila M. Ivanova

Aurora Art Publishers, Leningrad

Boris M. Pidemsky, Director
Toya Sokolova, Interpreter

Right: The Cabinet of Modes and Graces, 1758-1762. Portraits by Pietro Rotari. (*Peterhof.*)

INTRODUCTION

Every epoch leaves behind it a trail of clues for the social historian. Its buildings, its furnishings, its methods of transportation are all like so many fragments of a paper chase, by which the quarry can be run to earth even centuries later. But the most intimate clues—clothes, headdresses, hair styles, jewels—are also the most fragile pieces of evidence, which time blows away, and which often come down to us only through painting and sculpture. In this book we are fortunate enough to see a range of the clothes worn in Russia during the eighteenth and nineteenth centuries, at the court, in aristocratic and bourgeois circles, and at festivities in the villages. We can bring them to life by picturing the world in which they were worn: a world far from ours in its manners and customs, its climate and character.

The first to step on the stage is Peter the Great; which is as it should be, since he created modern Russia. Till he set his powerful stamp on the nation—forcing it to look West, and to take a leap into the eighteenth century—Russia had remained as in the Middle Ages. He himself disliked pomp. The houses he built for himself were modest and practical. His dining tables were on a scale to seat his family or his cronies. He was a skilled craftsman, and would receive an ambassador in his workshop, dressed in a carpenter's leather jerkin. Yet the wax figure of Peter at the Hermitage, sculpted by Carlo Rastrelli, father of the architect, is dressed in a suit of sky blue and silver brocade, the suit he wore for the coronation of his wife, whom he honored shortly before he died and who succeeded him as Catherine I. There could hardly be a stronger proof of the power of fashion than this dandified elegance for the ferocious, gigantic figure of the Tsar. (Andrew Swinton, who visited Russia in the late eighteenth century, remarked shrewdly of the wax figure of Peter, "It would have been more characteristic in iron.")

A social change which might seem small among Peter's tremendous upheavals had in fact an immense influence on Russian life. Until then, women had been kept in the *terem* —in purdah—seen only by their family and intimate friends, in their own homes. Dinners were exclusively for men, and were coarse, riotous, drunken gatherings. Peter introduced balls and masquerades, to which young girls as well as married women were invited. An enthusiastic English traveler wrote that "by teaching his bears to dance he rescued them from a savage state, and elevated to her natural sphere in society, the civilizer of man—Woman."

Throughout Russian history it is noticeable how frequently the pendulum of court atmosphere, and consequent social manners, swung between one reign and another. Peter's daughter Elizabeth was a very different character from her father, and she established a very different way of living. She appears to have inherited much of his prodigious energy; in her case, however, none of it was applied to affairs of state, but was poured into a round of perpetual pleasure. Balls, receptions, theatrical performances, banquets, and hunting parties followed one another in an endless stream. As a young woman she was a beauty, with a fine fresh complexion and large blue eyes. She was proud of her figure and of her slender legs, and enjoyed flattering them with the knee breeches worn by men at that period. The command went out for transvestite balls, which delighted Elizabeth and no doubt the young ladies of the court (and the young courtiers described by Mrs. Ward, after her residence in Petersburg in the 1730s, as being "just such things as mere pretty fellows are everywhere, viz., nothing, dressed fine") but were detested by the older ladies, and the older men, who tripped over their unaccustomed long skirts.

Just as her father had given orders for the adoption of Western-style dress, and her mother, Catherine I, had made rules for her modest assemblies (one of which was that no lady was to get drunk, and no gentleman before nine o'clock), so Elizabeth laid down a program of entertainment at court and the manner of dress that was to be worn. For example, on Sunday, court reception assembly day; on Monday, plays; on Tuesday, a masquerade ball; on Thursday, French comedy; and so on. The wearing of a Russian style for women — the caftan, a long tunic with a girdle at the waist — was decreed for evenings at the theater; and for the masquerade balls a domino with lace, and a small farthingale. The men were to wear colorful brocades. Elizabeth herself possessed so many dresses that fifteen thousand were said to have been found in her closets when she died. She would change two or three times during one evening, and woe betide any lady whose dress too nearly resembled that of the Empress; the unfortunate creature would be sent home in disgrace.

Elizabeth was, however, by no means an empty-headed doll. She had her father's passion for architecture (though her love of opulence was the antithesis of his simplicity), and one consequence of her brilliant scale of entertainment was her enthusiastic patronage of Bartolomeo Rastrelli, the architect best able to give her the settings she needed — and, many would say, the greatest architect who ever worked in Russia. For her he converted the modest buildings which were the early Winter Palace, the first country house at Tsarskoe Selo, and Le Blond's original Peterhof, into vast and splendid palaces. Their baroque exteriors have all been restored to their former beauty, but the elaboration and size of Rastrelli's greatest interiors have so far given pause even to the Soviet architect-decorators, who have faithfully restored so much. The huge Rastrelli ballroom and the Amber Room at Tsarskoe Selo are reported to be nearly ready for unveiling; but no clue has yet been found to the whereabouts of its famous amber paneling, which once gave the light a unique honey-colored glow, and which the Germans carried off in the War. Meanwhile one must be content with the Jordan Staircase and the Cathedral in the Winter Palace, and the Knights' Dining Room at Tsarskoe Selo.

To Elizabeth also (together with one of her many lovers, the cultured and gifted Count Ivan Shuvalov) must be given the credit for introducing the theater to St. Petersburg; so greatly did its citizens take to this form of art and entertainment that, to the present day, plays, opera, and ballet have played a greater part in the life of Russia than in that of any other country.

The pendulum swung once more when Elizabeth, after the brief reign of her nephew, Peter III, was succeeded by his wife, Catherine II — the Great. Her taste was again of a wholly different kind. At a time when rulers and aristocrats in all European countries accepted and enjoyed life in the full blaze of publicity (even to the levees, when people gathered to watch them dress), Catherine showed the originality and strength of her character by dividing her life firmly into its public and private aspects. Magnificent balls and receptions were still given, when she thought it to be appropriate; and on gala days she would dress as an empress, in trained robe and crown, and dine in splendor sitting on her throne and waited on by the great nobles. But she much preferred the private life that she created for herself, with the help of her architects: the life of the Hermitage, her retreat in the center of the Winter Palace, to which she invited writers, *savants*, and close friends. It was there that she kept her growing collection of paintings and sculpture, books, gems, and curiosities, which formed the substantial nucleus of the present Hermitage collection.

At Tsarskoe Selo, also, she felt it impossible to live as Elizabeth had done, among crowds of courtiers in the overwhelming decor of Rastrelli's halls; so she engaged the Scottish architect Charles Cameron to design for her a series of intimate suites: which he did, decorating them deliciously, to her great and warmly expressed pleasure.

"Hermitage" originally meant "a retreat," and that was exactly what Catherine sought. It was a blessed retreat from the ubiquitous courtiers and servants, for machinery was installed by which dishes ordered were sent up from the kitchens below, through trapdoors, without a servant setting foot in the room. (Peter the Great's "Hermitage" still stands in Peterhof park; but that is simply a dining room, made private by the same methods—not a series of beautifully furnished halls like Catherine's.) There, at least, people could speak freely, among friends they trusted. There all was simplicity and informality, enforced by the ten rules which Catherine herself wrote out and hung up: "Rules by which all who enter these doors must conduct themselves," and which included, "To leave every kind of rank at the door," "To dispute without warmth or passion," "To sit, stand, to walk about, as each thinks proper"—something ordinarily unthinkable in other court circles of any era. There were penalties for breaking the rules, and if all ten were broken the offender would never again be admitted.

There was another aspect of public and private life which Catherine skillfully kept apart: that was in respect of her lovers, of which she had a long succession. Of these, only Potemkin took any part in affairs of state, and he was a man of exceptional qualities, who deserved his position. Though their love affair lasted only two years, their friendship and collaboration lasted until his death, and she left it to him to choose all her subsequent lovers. All knew their place except the last, Platon Zubov, who exploited his position in a way which Catherine would never previously have tolerated.

Catherine loved the theater; but, again, she preferred the private theater that Giacomo Quarenghi built for her in the Winter Palace. Here, the audience was specially invited, and she herself occasionally wrote a play to be performed there. She confessed to having no ear for music, so the opera, which had begun to flourish under Elizabeth, meant nothing to her. Her ideas of dress were simple, except on state occasions. By birth a German princess, she studiously cultivated all things Russian. She introduced a graceful, simple Russian style of dress, often in white, sometimes in purple, in soft silk (brocade fell from favor). It was of a pinafore cut, over a blouse; and she wore her fur coats shaped in to the waist. Her jewels usually consisted of several rows of pearls. Later in life, she liked the Moldavian type of caftan, loose at the waist, and a Hungarian-style fur hat with tassels. Even in old age, in cap and dressing gown, she is reported as "preserving her majesty" by her upright carriage and firm step. Her lack of interest in ostentation was remarked on in several memoirs; she is described, for instance, as going out at night in the streets of Petersburg in an open carriage, with a very small suite, and "even when she visits the Senate,

Mikhail Romanov, the first Romanov Tsar, with his Privy Council, receiving a foreign embassy in the Throne Room of the Kremlin. Adam Olearius, 1719.

she has only 2 lackeys behind her carriage." C. F. P. Masson wrote, after her death, "The young persons of her court…regretted the happy evenings of the Hermitage, and that freedom of ease and pleasure which Catherine knew so well how to inspire; and they contrasted with these the military constraint and etiquette that were likely to succeed." One might as well say, "were bound to succeed," for Paul detested his mother. She had never allowed him the smallest part in government, although he was forty-three at her death, and he revenged himself by dismissing those she had employed, by stabling his soldiers in the Tauride Palace which she had built for Potemkin, and by generally making life at court as different as possible.

Paul was a rigid disciplinarian, and all court procedures were stiffened up. No one spoke or moved unless the Emperor did so first. He had no use for the picturesque or the luxurious, and gaiety was foreign to his nature. Uniforms and military drill were his passion; all such parades acquired additional splendor. The German traveler H. F. von Storch, who visited Russia at the turn of the century, remarked bitterly that, so far from finishing the most useful works begun by his mother, such as the quays and canals of Petersburg, and the highways, "the edifices he erects in greatest number are houses for exercising his soldiers in, barracks, guard-houses, and above all things, sentry boxes. Happily all these buildings are of wood, and will scarcely last longer than their builder." After only four years on the throne Paul was assassinated in his newly constructed Mikhailovsky Castle—

Reliquary, said to contain a nail that pierced Christ. Uspensky Cathedral, Moscow, fifteenth century. (*Drevnosti Rossiiskago Gosudartsva* [Moscow, 1849-1853.])

Icon: Feast of the Intercession of the Virgin. Novgorod, late fifteenth century. (*A La Vieille Russie.*)

Feast of the Holy Trinity, Moscow. Olearius, 1719.

Mikhail Feodorovich, Tsar or Grand Duke of
Moscow. Olearius, 1719.

Bell Tower of Ivan Veliki. Olearius, 1719.

Right: Church of the Resurrection·in the Kremlin of Rostov Veliki, 1670.

unmourned by any except his devoted wife, Maria Feodorovna, and his mistress, Lopukhina.

He was succeeded by the eldest of his four sons, Alexander I, who had been Catherine's favorite grandchild. A remarkably handsome man of personal charm, neither he nor his wife had any liking for social life. The responsibility for the war against Napoleon hung heavily on him. He undertook much traveling, to inspect his domains and to attend international congresses. He had strong religious leanings, and he and his wife were made melancholy by their childlessness. Mrs. C. A. A. Disbrowe, wife of the British Minister Plenipotentiary at the Court of St. Petersburg during Alexander's reign, wrote, "social life has declined," "the Court seldom receives," but added, "There are shooting parties here, from bears to sparrows." But the noble families made up for the court's neglect by staging more, and more elaborate entertainments than ever before. Mrs. Disbrowe writes of "*charades en action*," tableaux, comedies, which were performed sometimes by amateurs and sometimes by professional serf troupes. In writing home she says, "I wish heartily some of you young folks were at hand to partake of the excessive dissipation in which I am just now launched. Three balls in one week, and four for the next, is more than my age and condition deserve, but I have a remarkably young fit upon me just now, and I can dance at a great rate when I get partners."

The lives of Alexander I and his empress, Elizabeth Alexeevna, ended tragically and early. The Emperor took his ailing wife to Taganrog, on the Caspian Sea, but it was he who died there first, aged only forty-eight; his wife died a few weeks later. Having no direct heir, he was succeeded by his brother, Nicholas I—a disciplinarian and militarist like their father, Paul, but an abler and more balanced man, of tireless energy. He laid down rules for everything: the three or four designs which were to be used by the proprietors of country estates who wanted to build in the fashionable neoclassical style; the authors, from Aristotle onward, whose works could no longer be allowed into Russia because they mentioned the word "liberty." He turned up at rehearsals of the corps de ballet of the Imperial Theater, and took a hand in their training. His word was law—even in the case of the young lady who was abducted from her home by an officer, but later brought back; Nicholas announced, "This young person is a virgin."

During his reign social life at the Winter Palace reached, and even surpassed, its old brilliance. Horace Vernet, in a letter of 1843, wrote of an imperial ball, "It was magnificent; one was literally thrusting one's way through diamonds, one stepped over pearls and rubies; it had to be seen to be believed." Uniforms were no longer drab or forbidding. Officers of the Guard wore breeches of white cloth, silk stockings, silver-buckled shoes, and carried plumed tricornes—black for the infantry and white for the cavalry. For the women, Nicholas laid down that they should wear a Russian national dress of white silk with a red velvet bodice, a long train richly embroidered, and the *kokochnik* (headdress), also in red velvet, sewn with real or fake jewels. The great court ladies wore on the left breast a miniature of the Empress, framed in diamonds. (Prince Kurakin, who had large estates, adopted his own version of this custom. The women of his circle who had proved agreeable mistresses carried his portrait on their bosoms; those who had failed to please him were condemned to wear the same portrait on their backs, even when going to church, at which all the other ladies would titter.)

However much the social atmosphere at court swung from extravagance to sobriety and back again, and however much successive tsars and empresses decreed, and themselves wore, Russian styles of dress, society, outside the court, went its own way. Its manner of dressing became increasingly close to that of Paris, and its extravagance was diminished, in individual cases, only by reason of bankruptcy.

The memoirs and letters of travelers throughout the eighteenth and nineteenth centuries show that they are, without exception, struck by the lavishness of Russian hospitality, the size of their households, the richness of their furnishings, clothes, jewels, and carriages. Travelers in those days were not like the tourists of today, flying here and there, segregated in international hotels and scarcely meeting the natives of the countries they visit. Travel, then, could not be undertaken lightly; and the hardships of the journey made for a long stay on arrival. No one set out without being armed with introductions to people well placed in the society of the country they were to visit. In Russia, one introduction inevitably led to another; all those whose writings have come down to us were welcomed into numerous households, and many were presented at court. In reading them, therefore, one is taken inside a whole section of Russian life: a section not large in numbers, in comparison with the mass of the population, but overwhelming in its wealth and influence. Also, while moving in those circles, the interested visitor had time and opportunity to observe the manners and dress of other members of society, and note them for our benefit. Here then are some of the things we learn from contemporary accounts.

The visitor invited to the house of a Russian nobleman was first astonished at the crowd of carriages. "It would indeed puzzle a London coachman," said A. B. Granville in 1827, "to get up to the door during a grand rout, where probably 400-600 carriages-and-four arrive, and many of them remain in waiting." "A hundred attendants," wrote J. G. Kohl in 1842, "are allotted to the grand staircase alone.... The servants always appear in new liveries, made expressly for the occasion. Fifty of these staircase lackeys were dressed in purple velvet laced with silver, and fifty in crimson with gold. On the steps stood alternately an orange or lemon tree and one of these attendants." "A single dinner or ball," he notes, "often causes a house to put on a new face.... Palaces, in short, are put together with a rapidity that can be compared only to that with which theatrical decorations are arranged."

All the rooms would be superbly decorated. Early in the eighteenth century, in the time of Peter the Great and of Empress Elizabeth, there was much use of carved gilded wood for paneling and staircases and furniture, but as time went on even the simplest objects began to be made in costly materials. The discovery of quantities of semiprecious stones in the Urals made everyone who could afford them long to use them. Walls were ornamented with porphyry, amethyst, jade, jasper, and agate; furniture was decorated with gilded bronze; vases and dinner services were made of glass as well as of porcelain—and there were periods when nothing but silver was good enough for plates and goblets.

As for the food, Shoberl, in 1822, remarked that it appeared to be the greatest pride of the rich in Russia to surmount the difficulties of the climate by a prodigal use of hothouses, or by having grapes and melons brought from Astrakhan. "They strive," he said, "to cheat themselves into a belief that they reside in one of the southern countries of Europe.... Green peas and asparagus are as common in Moscow about Christmas as potatoes and cabbages in other countries." It was considered elegant to serve several kinds of wine; and a list would be put on the guests' plates, so that they could choose. The menus were remarkable: two kinds of soup, with the favorite Russian *piroghi* (pastry stuffed with rice and hard-boiled eggs, cabbage, mincemeat, or fish); *kulebiaka* (whole boned chickens wrapped in a delicate crust); caviar; cold ham; turkeys roasted with plums or nuts; geese with salted lemon; puddings with various types of sauce.

The Comte de Ségur, in the 1780s, remarked that well-to-do merchants loved to entertain their guests with excessive richness. "They serve enormous joints of beef, game, fish, eggs, pâtés, all at the same time and in such abundance that even the bravest stomach cries out for mercy." A lady who described herself as *An Englishwoman in Russia* in the mid-nineteenth century remarked on the refreshments loaded on tables at a ball given for the marriage of a merchant's daughter: "Immense cakes, trays of fruit, preserves, bonbons etc., twenty times as much as it was possible to require. Our host and hostess appeared never so pleased as when they saw us eating; indeed they seemed to expect us never to leave off for a single instant from the time of our arrival to that of our departure."

And what of the kitchens that produced food of such quality and in such profusion? No doubt the merchants' cooks would have been Russians; but foreign cooks, especially from France and Germany, were imported to teach the Russian servants—and kept on, in charge—in the great houses. R. Lyall, in 1816, tells us that "in some of the larger establishments of the nobles, four, six, eight and even above ten men cooks are employed, besides half-a-dozen, a dozen or a score of assistants."

When it comes to describing the dress of the men and women, richness is still the quality that most astonishes the visitors. The same Englishwoman quoted above wrote shrewdly, "No people value exterior appearance as much as they do. Mirrors hold the same position in Russia as clocks do in England; with us time is valuable, with them, appearance." Prince Stcherbatov is quoted as saying that, in the eighteenth century, clothes represented a capital expenditure almost equal to that of all other possessions. "Clothes" would, of course, have included furs and jewels: the first necessitated by the climate, and the second by the passion felt for them by men and women of all classes. Visitors were dazzled by the diamonds: men wore diamond buttons, shoe buckles, sword hilts, epaulettes, and star decorations; women wore them not only as jewelry but sewn into the embroidery of their dresses. Diamonds are most often remarked upon, by reason of their brilliance, but rubies and emeralds were not far behind; and pearls were massed on headdresses: real pearls for the rich, river pearls or pearl beads for those of modest means. "The richness of the clothes," wrote another contemporary, "passes all belief; there is nothing but brocade, velvet, smothered with embroidery in silver and silk. The wardrobe of a courtier or a fop were worth a fortune, and even those of modest people were always richly ornamented." Another aspect of dress noticeable in Russia was the widespread custom of wearing uniforms. All young men of good family spent some years in one of the crack regiments, and one reads that in 1740 it was laid down precisely what cloth each rank was to wear, and what it was to cost.

The statistics that tumble from the pens of the travelers stun the reader even more than those far larger sums that now fill the columns of our newspapers: for these last are the expenditure of governments on all manner of things undreamed of in earlier ages, while the travelers' statistics deal with the expenses and households of individuals. One is also powerfully, if vaguely, aware of the value that money had in those days, as compared

All the costumes shown in the following color plates were photographed in the Winter Palace.

Uniform of Catherine the Great as Colonel of the Life Guard Mounted Regiment, 1771. In the Hall of the Coats-of-Arms, designed by V. P. Stasov.

Costumes of the second half of the nineteenth century. In the Malachite Room, designed by A. P. Bryullov. At left: Uniform of a senator with the sash of the Order of Saint Andrew. In the center: Court dress of a *frelina* (from *Fräulein*), an unmarried young lady-in-waiting. There were approximately two hundred and fifty frelinas, daughters of high dignitaries, who served from the age of eighteen until marriage. On the left shoulder they wore the initials of the reigning empress in diamonds on a blue ribbon of the Order of Saint Andrew. At right and opposite: Court dress of the type worn by a member of the Imperial Family or by a lady-in-waiting of the highest order. There were approximately five hundred of these ladies-in-waiting. The rank of the wearer dictated the length of the train. Trains of the Imperial Family were carried by two pages from the Imperial School of Pages, those of the nobility by an attendant. A *kokochnik* of pearls and diamonds with tulle veil and long white kid gloves were worn with this type of gown. At court weddings, cloth-of-silver dresses like this were worn by women of the Imperial Family and their attendants.

Above: Costumes of the late eighteenth century, on the Jordan Staircase by Rastrelli, restored by Stasov after the fire of 1837. At left: Gentleman's court costume, 1780. In the center: Court dress of the seven-year-old future Alexander I, 1784. At right: Noblewoman's gala dress.

Right: Costumes of Peter the Great, early eighteenth century. At left: Cavalry uniform. In the center: Brocade dressing gown. At right: Court costume.

Costumes of the first half of the nineteenth century, in the private apartments of Nicholas II.

Right: In the Billiard Room. At left: Tulle ball gown embroidered with steel plaquettes from Tula, and shawl with a double-faced woven border, 1820. At right: Taffeta dress, 1820.

Above and right: In the Corner Drawing Room: Court dress of Dowager Empress Maria Feodorovna, widow of Paul I, 1820.

Opposite: Taffeta ball gown with straw embroidery, 1840.

with today. For example, the clever young men who called themselves "Les Deux Français dans le Nord de l'Europe" in the 1790s wrote of Potemkin — briefly the lover of Catherine the Great, and for years her friend, first minister, and outstanding general — "In 1791, during a stay of four or five months in Petersburg, he spent 1,200,000 roubles. He has been known to reserve in advance all the cherries from a tree in a hothouse, and to pay 5 roubles each for them. He possesses an immense quantity of jewels...and amuses himself pouring them from one hand to another like a child." Count Shuvalov, in the reign of Elizabeth, had an *income* of four hundred thousand rubles, but he spent on such a scale that he owed the crown more than a million at his death. Count Stroganov is reported as having six hundred servants in his palace in Petersburg, and Count Razumovsky nearly a thousand. The Sheremetev and Stroganov families each possessed forty thousand to fifty thousand serfs. Coming down to minor matters, a single bonnet made of cloth of gold, sewn with pearls, could cost twenty thousand francs (many clothes were imported from France).

There were houses in Petersburg where the food and wine alone cost a hundred thousand rubles a year, for the host might have twenty people at table, twice a day, and on special occasions each cover could cost several hundred rubles.

That such lavishness was a national, and not merely a class, characteristic can be learned both from literature and reportage. The modest land-owning family of Tatiana in Pushkin's *Eugene Onegin* spent far above their means on entertainment, wishing to attract suitors for their daughters, and then took all their belongings on an eight-day drive to Moscow, to spend a costly season there for the same purpose. Even more surprising is that the same spirit was shown by the peasants. J. A. Atkinson, who spent several of the early years of the nineteenth century in Russia, and who dedicated the resulting book to Alexander I, says of the female peasants, "They are hospitable and good managers, and frugal even to parsimony, yet extremely fond of show and ostentation, and will sometimes expend on an entertainment more than would keep them and their families decently for half a year." Village fêtes were occasions for tremendous celebration, in eating, drinking, singing, dancing — and dressing. Richly colored and embroidered clothes and *kokochniks* would be brought out of closets: though, as styles for the muzhik and his *baba* remained the same throughout this period, clothes worn so seldom would last a lifetime and even be passed down from one generation to another.

Above all, the money spent by the nobility on gambling was astronomical. Lyall, in 1816, remarked that the Russians "love light occupations and amusements, as plays, operas, masquerades, exhibitions, dancing, singing and instrumental music; chess, and draughts, and billiards; but above all, playing at cards, to which whole days, and weeks, and months, and years, are devoted." Playing at cards meant gambling, and for very high stakes. The younger brother of Platon Zubov, Catherine II's last lover, was able to stake thirty thousand rubles on a single card at faro. A writer in 1855 reported that a man who once possessed fourteen thousand serfs lost them all at cards. The Comte de Ségur, at a ball in a country house, found himself in his host's study, "where they played a hellish game — faro. What gold! What banknotes! People staked all they possessed." In a story by Lermontov, a colonel loses everything at the gambling table, then asks permission to play one more card — with his wife as the stake.

In the Picket Room by Stasov: At left: Ball gown of Natasha Alexandrovna Suvorov, c. 1810 At right: Uniform of her father, the great Field Marshal Alexander Vasilievich Suvorov.

From these habits of enormous expenditure and gambling arose a government institution called the Lombard. It was in a fashionable part of Petersburg and was a glorified pawnshop. On small items, for which there would be a ready sale if they were not reclaimed, the Lombard might lend half the value; on diamonds (which were sometimes brought in settings worth thirty thousand rubles), they would lend a third or a quarter only. They had to give up taking carriages as pledges, since they had not enough room to hold them, but land and houses could be pledged at an interest rate of six percent. The turnover of the Lombard was estimated at forty-five million rubles a year: Maria Feodorovna, widow of Paul and mother of Alexander I and Nicholas I, who held many charitable and public offices, directed it for a number of years.

One has only to follow the fortunes of the Rostov family in *War and Peace* to realize how fatally easy it was for the value of great estates to be eroded over the years, to the owners' astonishment—because they never made any calculations, but spent whatever they and their wives, their sons, and their daughters thought desirable. There was so much rivalry among the noblemen, and parsimony—or even prudence—was so foreign to their nature, and would have been so much despised, that each family constantly strove to outshine the other. Here is J. G. Kohl: "As not only the mistress of the house, as well as the master, has her own coachman, postillion, and team of four horses, but it is customary in many families for the children to have their own carriages...it is easy to conceive that such a number of horses, carriages and coachmen might be taken for the establishment of a sovereign prince."

Of course, horses and carriages were to them what cars are to us, but they had a far wider and more tempting range of costly possibilities. Riders wanted English or Arab horses. For carriage work a perfectly matched pair would be the minimum requirement, and we have heard that several sets of four horses might be considered necessary for a family to drive in style. To the wealthy, the grass in other fields is always greener. Russian carriages were despised, so ornate equipages were imported from France and Holland. The winter conditions, lasting for four or five months of the year, made sleighs a necessity—and were another source of expense. Shoberl reported, in 1822, that the sleighs were always gaudy, "decorated with red, green, gold and silver, strange carved work and whirligigs of iron. The sledges of the nobles are very handsome; lined with furs, and with an apron of green or crimson velvet, bordered with gold lace." Altogether, winter was a wonderful time. Visitors wrote marveling, "Cold to the Russians seems to be what heat is to the torpid animals," and "The extreme cold of winter, which benumbs all nature, seems on the contrary to give fresh elasticity to all the faculties of the Russians. They sing, they laugh, they wrestle, tumbling about like great bears among the snow."

One engaging aspect of Russian hospitality was the way that it could embrace a far wider circle than friends, or friends of friends. The tsars and empresses had always set an example by giving two enormous entertainments to the public each year. On New Year's Eve they kept open house at the Winter Palace, and up to thirty thousand guests of all classes streamed in, to fill those vast and innumerable rooms, which blazed with chandeliers. On July 1 they kept open house at Peterhof, about twelve miles from Petersburg. This was on a far larger scale, for the great park could swallow up a hundred and fifty thousand people. Many accounts have been given of this fête. The roads were choked with carriages, which were used for dressing and sleeping. People stayed all night, because the day ended with a splendid display of fireworks, at which the Russians excelled. At that time of year, during the White Nights, there is no darkness. Remarkably enough, it is always noted that the crowds on both these occasions behaved perfectly, with no pushing or shoving, and no great noise. It would be said acidly that nothing of the sort would be possible in London or Paris.

A number of the nobles followed the imperial example. Large as their palaces were, they could not literally keep open house in them, but in the summer months those with estates in the country, near the cities—and especially those with estates on islands in the Neva—would throw them open to the public (without charge) and provide refreshments, bands, dancing, sailing, fishing, swinging (a favorite Russian pastime), and playing bowls; and again the evening would end with fireworks. *Scenes in Russia* (1814) describes how "a friendly invitation in four languages, inscribed over the entrance to the grounds, authorizes everyone of decent appearance and behaviour to amuse himself there."

As one reads these descriptions of Russian life one catches the sense of excitement, the glimpse of Arabian Nights splendor, and especially the foreign strangeness of the scene. The wealthy and cultivated could move between the capitals of Western Europe without noticing much to cause them surprise; but one feels that the most sophisticated Westerners are caught off their guard in Russia. Most are in ecstasies, but some are shocked at strange customs, and some are amused. Many visitors were impressed by the talent as well as the beauty of the women and the young girls. More time seems to have been devoted to their cultural education than to that of their menfolk. They are described as speaking four or five languages, and being familiar with the works of the best writers in those languages. They were also able to play several instruments.

Another way in which the Russians were conspicuously civilized was in their habit of taking baths. At a time when Western Europe was doing primitive things with water cans, Russians enjoyed the Finnish sauna. Jean Chappe d'Auteroche in 1770 wrote, "These baths were in use all over Russia; every inhabitant of this vast tract of land, from the sovereign to the meanest subject, bathes twice a week, and in the same manner. Every individual, even of the smallest fortune, has a private bath in his own house, in which the father, mother and children sometimes bathe all together." For those who had not "even the smallest fortune" there were public baths of the same type. Prints exist, showing men and women, naked amid wreaths of steam, being beaten with twigs, and plunging into icy pools, in the time-honored manner.

Their vast country, vast fortunes and estates, vast households of serfs, made the Russian imperial families and nobility somewhat larger than life; and their vitality also appeared boundless. Of course, few of them had anything to do except enjoy themselves. It is clear that they hardly knew how to pass their time or spend their money. Hence the constant search for new games to play—which led to that most spectacular of pre-machine-age roller coasters, Katalnaya Gorka. Hence the innumerable precious trinkets that they gave one another, such as the pair of solid gold bears in the Hermitage Treasury, whose little mouths glitter with diamond teeth, and the spate of jeweled eggs at Easter.

Madame de Staël as usual put her finger on an intrinsic ingredient of the Russian character: "The chief characteristic of this nation is something gigantic in every way: ordinary measurements simply do not apply to them. I do not wish to suggest that true greatness or stability are not to be found among them; but the boldness, the imagination of the Russians knows no bounds; with them everything is colossal rather than proportionate; daring rather than deliberate; and if the target is not hit, it is because it has been overshot."

Audrey Kennett

Triumphal Arrival of the Swedish Galleys Seized on May 30, 1719, at Vassilievsky Island, St. Petersburg. A. F. Zubov, 1719.

PETER I

1682-1725

Peter the Great was born in 1672, the youngest child of the Tsar Alexis and his second wife, Natalya Narishkin. At the age of ten he was made joint Tsar with his imbecile half-brother, Ivan V, under the regency of his half-sister, Sophia. Nevertheless, he spent his boyhood in virtual exile, growing up in a suburb of Moscow with aristocratic and peasant companions, whom he organized in military maneuvers and who eventually became the first members of Peter's famous Semenovsky and Preobrazhensky regiments. He spent much time in the foreign settlement near Moscow, and from craftsmen there learned some twenty trades, which he practiced throughout his life, including printing, carpentry, cabinet making, sailing, firework manufacture, and the sciences of fortification and artillery fire. In 1689, with the aid of the Streltsi, semi-military formations in Moscow, he overthrew Sophia and assumed personal rule.

Russia was almost continually at war under Peter. In order to secure access to the Baltic and Black Seas, he fought Ottoman Turkey (1695-1696), and in the Great Northern War with Sweden he defeated Charles XII in the Battle of Poltava. His ambition and greatest accomplishment was to bring Russia into the European sphere. After touring the Continent incognito during 1697 and 1698, he returned home at the news of a military revolt and took drastic vengeance on his opponents.

To modernize society, Peter personally cut off the beards of his boyars and ordered them to replace their long robes and conical hats with Western dress inspired by the court of Louis XIV. He then founded the capital city of St. Petersburg on the Baltic marshes (at a cost of human life comparable to the building of the pyramids), introduced Western technology, and completely changed the Russian government and military system, increasing the power of the monarchy at the expense of the nobility and the Orthodox Church.

Right: Peter the Great, Emperor of all the Russias. Christian Fritzsch, 1685-1769.

A huge man six feet seven inches tall, cruel, crude, and devoted to Russia, Peter was a contradictory figure. Unhappy in his first marriage to Eudoxia Lopukhina, by whom he had a son, Alexis, whom he persecuted and had killed, he married in 1706 an illiterate Lithuanian servant, the mistress of his favorite Alexander Menshikov, and crowned her as his consort. They had three children, Anna Petrovna, Elizabeth, and a son, Peter, who died at the age of three in 1719. Peter I was succeeded by his wife, who, with the aid of Menshikov, was installed as Empress for two years (1725-1727) as Catherine I.

We conquer by water and by fire.

Motto of Peter I
on the first medal
struck in Russia

Myself a pupil; I seek teachers.

Motto of Peter I
on his personal seal

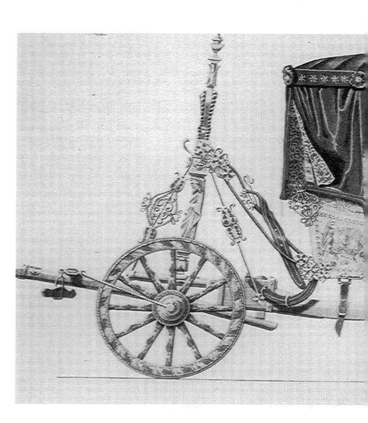

Right: A Tsar's Coach, late seventeenth century. (*Drevnosti.*)

Peter the Great. Engraving by E. Tehemesoff from the portrait by J. M. Nattier.

The Tsar...was very tall and might be called handsome; his countenance was beautiful but had something of the savage in it which put you to fear. His dress was of sailor fashion, coat altogether plain....

At table the Tsar placed himself near the Queen.... There took him very often a sort of convulsion like tic or St. Vitus, which it was beyond his power to control. That happened at table now. He got into contortions, gesticulations; and as the knife which was in his hand went dancing about within arm-length of the Queen, it frightened her, and she motioned several times to me. The Tsar begged her not to mind, for he would do her no ill; at the same time he grasped her by the hand, which he did with such violence that the Queen was forced to shriek out. This set him heartily laughing; saying she had not bones of so hard texture as his Catherine's.

WILHELMINA. aged nine,
sister of Frederick the Great of Prussia, 1717

Cavalry uniform of Peter I—blue broadcloth coat, red broadcloth breeches, silk-covered buttons, silver-thread trim. (*The Hermitage.*) (See page 22.)

The reign of Catherine I may be considered as the reign of Menshikov; that empress having neither the inclination nor abilities to direct the helm of government; and she placed the most implicit confidence in a man who had been the original author of her good fortune, and the sole instrument of her elevation to the throne. During her short reign her life was very irregular: she was extremely averse to business; would frequently pass whole nights in the open air; and was particularly intemperate in the use of tokay-wine.... She could neither read nor write.... Gordon...says, "She was a very pretty well-lookt woman, of good sense.... The great reason why the tzar was so fond of her, was her exceeding good temper; she never was seen peevish or out of humour; obliging and civil to all, and never forgetful of her former condition; withal, mighty grateful."

ARCHDEACON COXE, 1784

Catherine I, Empress of Russia, second wife of Peter I. Engraving by Houbraken from the portrait by J. M. Nattier.

Left: Seventeenth-century Moscow woman's court costume, made for a nineteenth-century masquerade. (*The Hermitage.*)

With the help of an orderly I penetrated to the Emperor's workshop, where I found him dressed in a leather jerkin like a workman, operating a lathe. He adored this work. In his mastery he could compete with the best turners, and he could also carve portraits and figures. During my visit, he from time to time left the lathe, walked to and fro, and discussed the most important affairs.

Danish Ambassador to the Court of Peter I

Dressing gown of Peter I, of imported brocade, early eighteenth century. (*The Hermitage.*)

Above and at right: Field caftan of Peter I. (*The Kremlin.*) Cranberry-colored silk of Russian manufacture, from Zakharina Pavlova, trimmed with gold lace from Western Europe, seventeenth century.

See, these things [sleeves] are in your way. You are safe nowhere with them. At one moment you upset a glass, then you dip them in the sauce. Get gaiters made of them.

PETER I, to boyars

Enamel portrait of Peter I by Musikiski. St. Petersburg, 1719. (*A La Vieille Russie.*)

Peter I's uniform of the Preobrazhensky Regiment—green broadcloth, red broadcloth cuffs; sash, denoting rank, of woven silver, blue, red, and gold. Tricorne not shown. Worn by Peter at the battle of Poltava. (*The Hermitage.*)

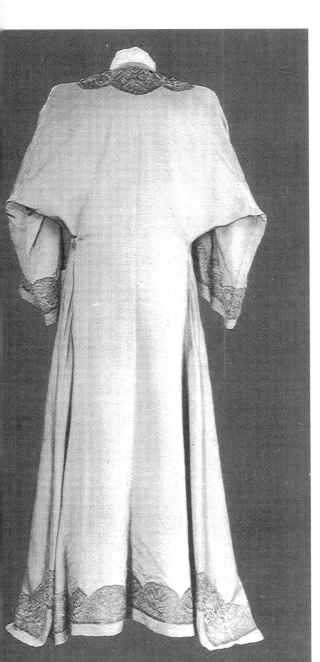

I would give one-half of my lands to learn of thee how to govern the other half.

PETER, at the grave of Richelieu

The Tsar inspected his troops at exercise; and seeing at a glance how backward they were...he went himself through all the attitudes and movements of the manual exercise, teaching them by his own motions how they should endeavor to form their heavy clumsy bodies. Tired at last with the uncouth horde, he went off with a bevy of Boyars to a dinner which he had ordered at his Ambassador Lefort's. Salvos of artillery mingled with the shouts of the drinkers, and the pleasures of the table were protracted to a late hour of the evening.

JOHANN KORB, 1698

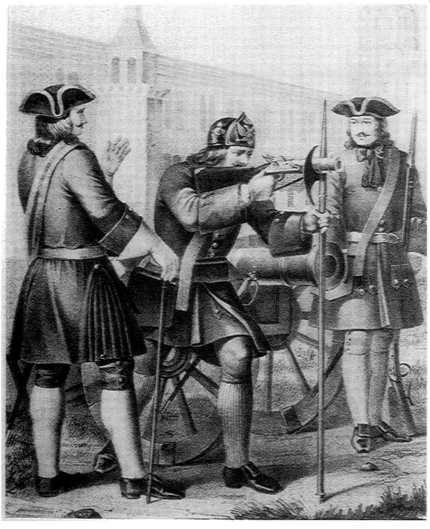

Officer, cannoneer, and musketeer of the Artillery Regiment, early eighteenth century. Viskovatov, 1844.

Left: The Grand Duke of Moscow and the Grand Khan of the Tatars, seventeenth-century engraving.

The Tsar is destroying the old customs and faith of his people; he is altering everything according to German methods and is creating a powerful army and fleet, thereby annoying everyone; sooner or later he will perish at the hands of his own subjects.

THE KHAN OF CRIMEA, to the Sultan of Turkey

Lancer of the Preobrazhensky Regiment, 1709. Viskovatov, 1844.

Helmet of a Grenadier Guard officer, 1705-1732. Viskovatov, 1844.

Wherever I see a streight avenue, I know that Peter has been here, and has cut some of the trees formerly growing where I now walk.... You may easily imagine that I feel myself a foot higher, in walking in a path which has been cleared for me by an Emperor!... Peter was never at ease in his robes: the hatchet and sword were always in his mind, and he sometimes forgot himself so far as to invite Ambassadors to assist him in cutting down trees for his Dock-Yards!

ANDREW SWINTON, writing of Peterhof, 1789

Seventeenth-century boyar's costume, made for a nineteenth-century masquerade. (*The Hermitage.*)

Above: Town of Samara, near the Volga. Olearius, 1719.

Below: Town of Colomna, near Moscow. Olearius, 1719.

Court costume of Peter I — frock coat, blue cord with silver lace; waistcoat, silver brocade, 1710-1720. (*The Hermitage.*)

We are in the Netherlands in good health and following God's word, thanks to God's blessing and your prayers. Being of Adam's line, we labor. We do not work of necessity but of good will for the sake of our sea routes, in order that having complete experience, we can, in the name of Jesus Christ, be conquerors, and liberators of the Christians. That, till my last breath, I shall not cease to desire.

PETER I, to the Patriarch Adrian

Right: Staff, seventeenth century. (*The Kremlin.*)

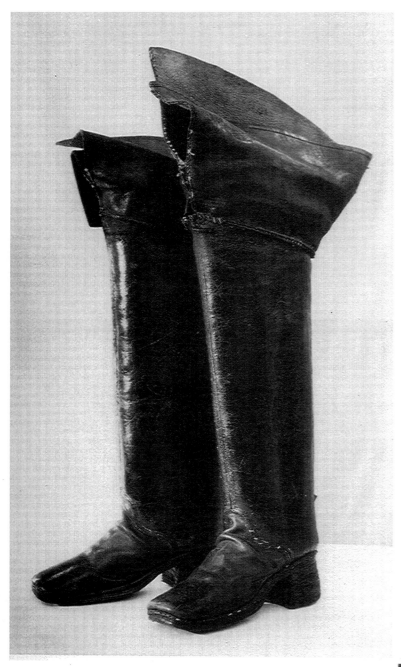

Reliquary casket of gold, with an enamel of Saint George and the dragon, containing the bones of a saint, eighteenth century. (*The Metropolitan Museum of Art.*)

Boots worn by Peter I. (*The Kremlin.*)

Brandenburgs of woven gold, with round gold buttons; closings for the front of a male costume, seventeenth century. (*The Kremlin.*)

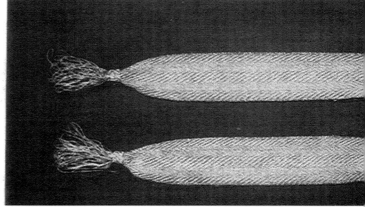

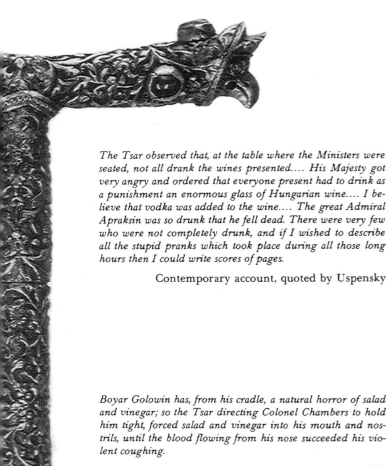

The Tsar observed that, at the table where the Ministers were seated, not all drank the wines presented.... His Majesty got very angry and ordered that everyone present had to drink as a punishment an enormous glass of Hungarian wine.... I believe that vodka was added to the wine.... The great Admiral Apraksin was so drunk that he fell dead. There were very few who were not completely drunk, and if I wished to describe all the stupid pranks which took place during all those long hours then I could write scores of pages.

Contemporary account, quoted by Uspensky

Boyar Golowin has, from his cradle, a natural horror of salad and vinegar; so the Tsar directing Colonel Chambers to hold him tight, forced salad and vinegar into his mouth and nostrils, until the blood flowing from his nose succeeded his violent coughing.

JOHANN KORB, 1700

A double standing covered drinking cup; silver, parcel-gilt. Moscow, 1745. (*The Metropolitan Museum of Art.*)

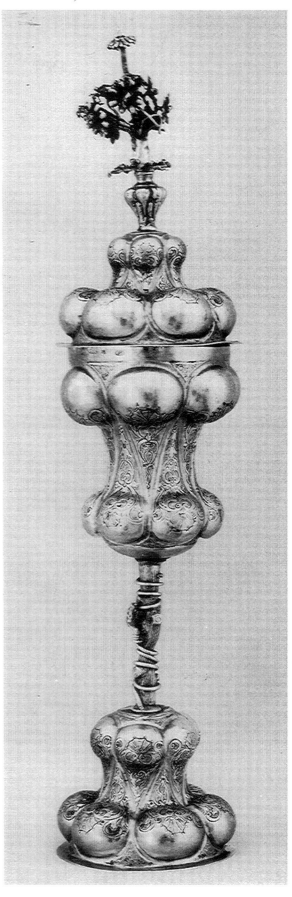

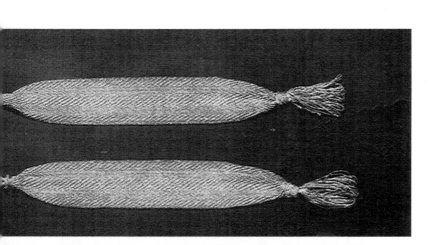

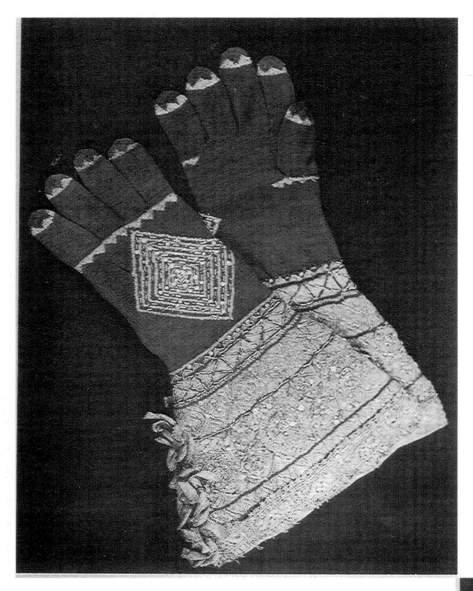

Gold-embroidered wool gauntlets, seventeenth
century. (*The Kremlin.*)

Pearl-embroidered boots, seventeenth
century. (*Drevnosti.*)

Shirinka, cloth used on an altar; white taffeta
embroidered with gold and pearls. (*Patriarch's
Collection, the Kremlin.*)

Red-velvet, pearl-embroidered lady's boot, second half of the seventeenth century. (*The Kremlin.*)

A Tatar woman, c. 1700. Lebrun.

House dress of the Patriarch Nikon, seventeenth century. K. W. Solntzev, 1869.

Easter procession at the Kremlin. Olearius, 1719.

On the morning of this Great Sunday of the Palms...the Patriarch Nicon descended from his palace wearing a mandys of green velvet, having for its emblems cherubim and seraphim in gold, pearls, and precious stones, embroidered with pearls and valuable red shells. His white latia (like the mitre on his head) was adorned with gold and precious stones. The "palms" were brought to him and he distributed them to the attendants and archons of the Emperor and to my master, the Patriarch of Antioch.... A procession was formed to go from the Kremlin down to the great group of many churches in one, the Cathedral built by Ivan the Terrible....

In front of the procession was the large tree, made of the branches brought by the country folk. It was hung with bunches of raisins, pieces of sugar, and apples. It was fastened on to two sledges on which rode six little choristers.... A horse, trained for its special duties and never ridden except on Palm Sundays, was brought for Patriarch Nicon to ride. The horse was covered with linen and the Patriarch sat on it in a velvet chair-shaped saddle, holding the cross in his right hand, the Gospel in his left, and blessing the assembled crowds.... The archons and great officers of State in jewelled robes of brocade walked on either side of him, while the Emperor's deputy took the bridle and led the horse, the procession following. (If the Emperor had been present he would have himself led the horse.) In front of the horse ran a hundred boys, sons of harquebusiers and guards. They were clad in cloaks from the Emperor's Treasury, green, blue, red, and yellow, and they vied with each other in spreading their cloaks under the horse's feet, then running forward to go through the same action again and again.

PAUL OF ALEPPO. *The Travels of Macarius, Patriarch of Antioch, 1655*

Shaven boyar removing his hat, by Peter's order, seventeenth century. Solntzev, 1869.

Crown of Empress Anna, 1730.

ANNA IVANOVNA

1730-1740

Daughter of the feebleminded Ivan V and a niece of Peter I, Anna, born in 1693, was married by Peter at the age of seventeen to Frederick William, the Duke of Courland. On their way home, the Duke died as a result of the lavish wedding festivities, and the widowed Anna lived on at Courland until she was chosen at the age of thirty-seven by the Supreme Privy Council to be Empress of Russia. The Council had hoped to gain power through her appointment, but her court was run by Baltic Germans, among them her favorite Ernst Biron, who ruthlessly oppressed the Russian nobility and made Anna's a reign of terror.

Uneducated, Anna remained a puppet of Russia, Prussia, and Poland throughout her life. She allied herself with the Emperor Charles VI of Austria and intervened in the War of the Polish Succession, attacking Turkey in 1736. Charles, however, made a separate peace with the Turks and forced Russia to do the same, forfeiting all her conquests with the single exception of Azov, a strategic fortress near the mouth of the River Don.

Anna's court was crude and vulgar. She employed dwarfs and freaks for entertainment and enjoyed mocking the traditional ceremonies and humiliating court personalities. To pay for her court extravaganzas and her wars, she relentlessly taxed the peasantry, but it is safe to say that every level of the Russian population resented her.

She chose the newborn son of her niece, Anna Leopoldovna, and the Duke of Brunswick to be her successor, and on the eve of her death she appointed Biron as regent of the child, who succeeded her as Ivan VI.

Coronation Medal of Empress Anna Ivanovna, "Empress Anna, Supreme Ruler of Russia, crowned in Moscow, April 28, 1730."

Throne of Tsar Mikhail Feodorovich, founder of the Romanov dynasty, placed in the Uspensky Cathedral and the Granovitaia Palace at coronation time. (*Drevnosti.*)

Empress Anna Ivanovna, Coronation Portrait, 1730.

Clowns at the court of Anna Ivanovna. Anna is at the left, reclining among courtiers. Clowns and dwarfs were accepted entertainment at court in eighteenth-century Russia.

The prince went first to the church with his court, with no great pomp. Then...the coaches of the people in posts under the government, and the nobility; their equipages were as fine as could be, both coaches and liveries...one, that I thought was as pretty as any, was, two running-footmen-negroes, dressed in black velvet, so exactly fitted to their bodies, that they appeared naked, only feathers put on after the Indian fashion. After all these were passed, came prince Charles, the duke of Courland's youngest son, in a chariot, with twelve footmen walking before, four running-footmen, two pages, and two gentlemen on horseback. Then prince Peter, his eldest brother, in the same manner. Then the duke, in a most magnificent chariot....

Then came her majesty and the bride, which was a procession of itself; first, came forty-eight footmen, twelve running-footmen, twenty-four pages, with their governor on horseback; second, the gentlemen of the bed-chamber, on horseback...; third, the lords of the bed-chamber on horseback, each with two running-footmen to lead the horse, and four servants with three led horses...; fourth, the master of the horse, attended by all the grooms, equerries, and riding-masters of her majesty's stables. 5th, The master of the buck-hounds, attended by all the officers of the hunt.... 6th, The under-marshal of the court with his staff. 7th, The great marshal with his staff.... 8th, The chariot, which was made to hold one person backwards, excessive rich, drawn by eight horses; in it the empress sat forward, and the bride backward. She was dressed in a stiffened bodied gown of silver stuff, embroidered with silver, the stomacher all diamonds, her own hair curled, with four tresses twisted with diamonds, and a little coronet of diamonds....

Saber and scabbard decoration, second half of the seventeenth century. (*Drevnosti.*)

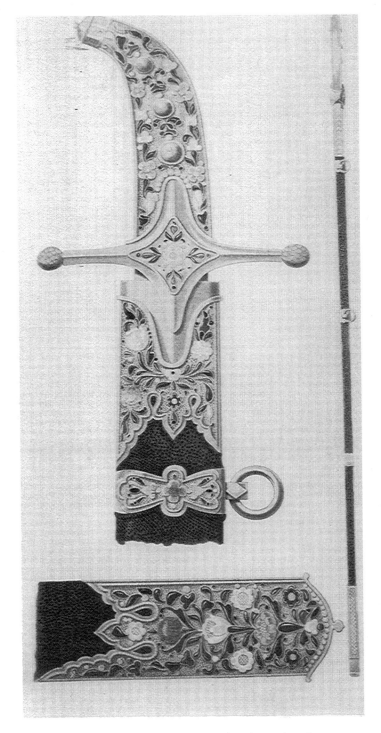

Friday, after dinner, there was a masquerade; there were four quadrilles, as they are called, consisting of twelve ladies each, besides the leader of each quadrille. The first was led by the bride and bridegroom, who were dressed in orange-coloured dominos, and little caps of the same, with a silver cockade, and a little laced ruff round the neck, tied with the same ribbon.... The second was led by the princess Elizabeth and prince Peter, in green dominos and gold cockades, and their twelve couple the same. The third by the dutchess of Courland and count Soltikoff (a relation of the empress) in blue dominos and pink and silver cockades. The fourth by her daughter and youngest son, in pink dominos and green and silver cockades.... There was a supper for the four quadrilles only, in the long gallery; the table had benches round it, so placed as to look like a turf bank, and the table the same; the table and benches were covered with moss and flowers, stuck in as if growing, and the supper, though very magnificent, was served to look like a rural entertainment. The empress walked about all the evening unmasked....

On Sunday there was a masquerade in the garden of the summer-palace, which was finely illuminated, and a firework in the river, which runs by the side of the garden.... And thus ended this grand wedding, from which I am not yet rested, and what is worse, all this rout has been made to tie two people together, who, I believe, heartily hate one another: at least, I think, one may answer for it, that is her case, and she showed it throughout all this week's feasting in a public shocking manner, and continues to treat him with the utmost contempt....

Letters from A Lady Who Resided Some Years in Russia...(Wedding festivities of Anna Leopoldovna, niece of Empress Anna, to Anton Ulrich of Brunswick, 1739)

Overleaf: The Chosen Fireworks Displayed at the Coronation Day of the Empress, Supreme Ruler of All the Russias, Anna Ivanovna, 1730.

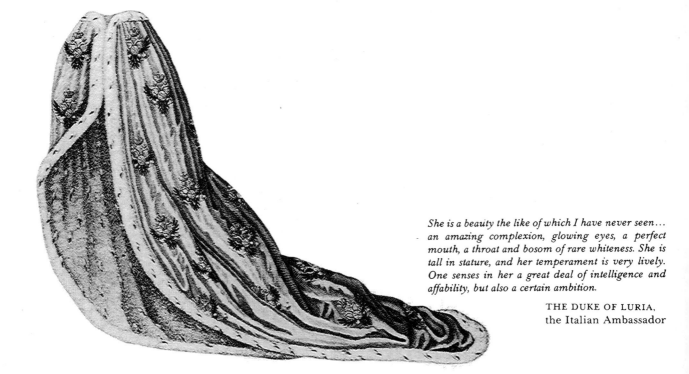

ELIZABETH

1741-1762

Born in 1709, Elizabeth was the favorite child of Peter I and Catherine I. Her father dreamed of marrying her to Louis XV of France, and she was brought up to speak French fluently. During the reign of Empress Anna, she was exiled to the countryside, where she led a robust life among the peasants and wore boy's clothing. Nevertheless, she grew up to become a voluptuous, self-assured woman with a great deal of personal charm and intelligence. When Anna Leopoldovna assumed the regency for her infant son, Ivan VI, and threatened to banish Elizabeth to a convent, the young woman seized power in a coup d'état with the help of the Shuvalov Brothers and the Preobrazhensky guards, with whom she was very popular.

Elizabeth, however, was more interested in organizing splendid court and church ceremonies than in governing the country. Although she was pious, she loved luxury and beauty and owned more than fifteen thousand magnificent Western European dresses. She hired the great architect Bartolomeo Rastrelli to build the Winter Palace in St. Petersburg and the Catherine Palace, named for her mother, at Tsarskoe Selo ("Tsar's Village," a few miles south of St. Petersburg). Like the empresses before her, Elizabeth made hers a reign of favorites. She built the Anichkov Palace for Cyril Razumovsky, her "Emperor of the Night" (and surely morganatic husband), and she encouraged Ivan Shuvalov to found the Academy of Arts and, with his friend the brilliant scientist-inventor Mikhail Lomonosov, to establish the first Russian university.

Guided by her trusted Chancellor, Alexis Bestuzhev-Ryumin, Elizabeth enhanced Russia's prestige as a major European power and tried to rid the country of the hated German influence, siding against Frederick the Great of Prussia in the Seven Years' War (1756-1763).

Above: The Coronation Robe of Her Imperial Highness, Elizabeth Petrovna, 1742.

Childless and anxious about the succession, she brought her nephew Peter of Holstein back to Russia and imported a German princess as his bride, the future Catherine the Great. At first she was kind to Catherine, even nursing her through a case of smallpox, but she soon became jealous, and when the unhappy couple finally had a child (who was to become Paul I) after nine years of marriage, Elizabeth took him from his parents and raised him herself, to the detriment of his health and sanity. When her German-loving nephew succeeded her as Peter III, he took Russia out of the Seven Years' War, making Frederick's ultimate victory possible.

Elizabeth in Coronation Dress. J. E. Nilson, 1785.

Grotto in the gardens of the Summer Palace, St. Petersburg. Bashutzski, 1834.

Below: Stove tile of tin-enameled earthenware, eighteenth century. (*The Metropolitan Museum of Art.*)

The Empress ordered Sumarokov's comedies played at Court. She took great pleasure in attending the performances, and it was soon observed that she watched with greater interest than might have been expected....

She took a particular pleasure in dressing the actors. She had magnificent clothes made for them, and they were covered with Her Majesty's jewels. It was noticed that the first lover, a rather handsome boy of eighteen or nineteen, was, as befitted him, the best dressed; and he was soon also outside the theater wearing diamond buckles, rings, watches, lace jabots and expensive linen.

When he left the Cadet Corps, the Master of the Hunt, Count Razumovsky...immediately made him his Aide de Camp.... The courtiers drew their own conclusions and decided that if Count Razumovsky had taken Cadet Beketov as his A.D.C., he could only be trying to balance the position of M. Shuvalov, the Gentleman of the Bedchamber.... So the impression grew that this young man was coming into great favor with the Empress....

[On Easter Sunday, 1750, Elizabeth] seemed to be in a very bad humor. It was whispered that this choleric disposition was caused by the embarrassment in which Her Majesty found herself among her four favorites, Razumovsky, Shuvalov, Kachinevsky and Beketov.... It must be admitted that anyone but Her Majesty would have been embarrassed with less than that. To deal with four men and conciliate them all is not a task that everyone could accomplish.

CATHERINE II, on Elizabeth

Right: Elizabeth, aged seven, by Louis Caravaque, in the Blue Chinese Drawing Room, Tsarskoe Selo.

Elizabeth is a prey to such terror that she rarely stays more than two days in the same place, and few people know where she sleeps.

LORD HYNDFORD, English Minister to the Court of Elizabeth

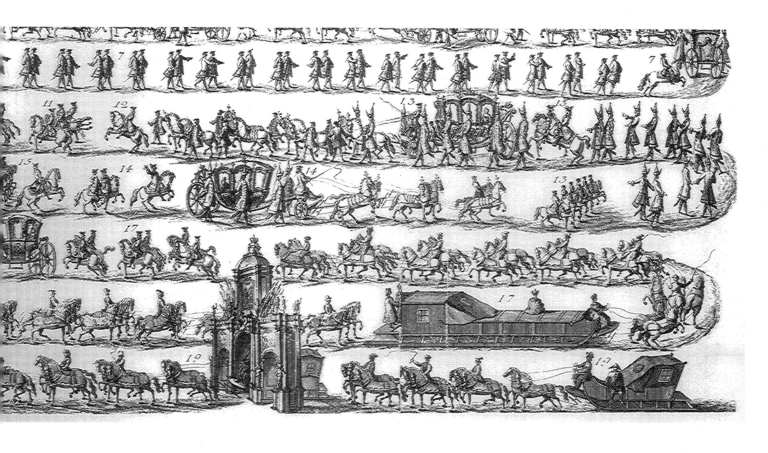

Ceremony of the Procession of Her Imperial Highness, the Empress Elizabeth, from the Kremlin Winter House to the Annenhoff Winter House, 1742.

For her coronation, Elizabeth and her court traveled by sleigh from St. Petersburg to Moscow, where all tsars were traditionally crowned. The sleighs of Imperial Russia could reach unimaginable proportions. For Catherine's trip to the south, Potemkin had built for her a miniature palace on runners, containing salon, library, and bedroom. In it eight people could pass abreast. It had six windows and was heated by porcelain stoves. The court followed in fourteen large sleighs and a hundred and eighty-four smaller ones.

Below: Court costume of Emperor Peter II, made in France; green broadcloth, gold embroidery. (*The Hermitage.*) Grandson of Peter I, half-nephew of Elizabeth, Peter II reigned from 1727 to 1730 and died of smallpox at fifteen.

This entertainment was essential at a Court where there was no conversation, where everybody cordially hated everybody else, where slander took the place of wit and any mention of politics was reported as lèse-majesté! Intricate intrigues were mistaken for shrewdness. Science and art were never touched on, as everybody was ignorant of those subjects; one could lay a wager that half the Court could hardly read and I would be surprised if more than a third could write.

CATHERINE II as Grand Duchess, on gambling and card playing at the Court of Elizabeth

Gentleman's court dress—frock coat of red broadcloth, with gold embroidery, silk waistcoat; late eighteenth century. (*The Hermitage.*)

Left: Brocade—purple, gold, and silver; silk and metal thread. Moscow, eighteenth century. Attributed to Marco Ciccani. (*The Metropolitan Museum of Art.*)

57

"So this was Petersburg...our Palmyra of the North."—Ivan Turgenev. The Neva Quai in 1778. Engraving after J.-B. Le Prince.

CATHERINE II

1762-1796

Princess Sophia of Anhalt-Zerbst, born in Germany in 1729, was brought to Russia at the age of fifteen by the Empress Elizabeth to marry her nephew, the future Peter III. The young bride, now Catherine, was neglected by her unstable husband and isolated at the court, but she read widely, especially Voltaire and Montesquieu, and learned a great deal about Russia. Peter III, after reigning for five months, had managed to alienate the power structure in the government through his outspoken love of Prussia and hatred of his own country; he was overthrown by Catherine and the Orlov brothers and assassinated six days later.

As Empress, Catherine led Russia into participation with the political and cultural forces of Europe, and bolstered the economy by expropriating wealth from the Church. She attempted to draw up a constitution and to emancipate the serfs, but, afraid of losing the support of the nobility, she eventually tightened restrictions on the serfs and extended serfdom to the Ukraine.

Catherine's Prime Minister, Grigori Potemkin, was her most influential counselor; he was the only one of her favorites to play a political role as well as a personal one (he even chose her companions, once their love affair had ended). Under his guidance she turned to expansion and in 1787 annexed the Crimea. She later participated in the division of Poland among Russia, Austria, and Prussia, and in all managed to extend Russian territory by two hundred thousand square miles, establishing its control over the Baltic and Black Seas, reorganizing twenty-nine provinces, and building a hundred new towns.

A woman of tremendous energy and intellectual curiosity, Catherine rose at five in the morning and worked fifteen hours a day. She corresponded with Voltaire, Diderot, d'Alembert, and others, and gained a considerable reputation in Europe for her enlightened attitudes. Her writings fill a five-foot shelf: memoirs, letters, a history of Russia, fairy tales, and allegories, as well as comedies, tragedies, adaptations of Shakespeare, masques, and comic operas for the Hermitage theater. She patronized the arts, encouraged the sciences (she submitted to vaccination as an example to her subjects), and founded schools for the nobility. Seven books a year were being published in Russia at the end of Peter I's reign; during Catherine's, eight thousand were published.

She built up the foremost art collection in Europe with the help of her agent, Baron Frederick Melchior von Grimm, and other advisers. By purchasing the Cobentzl, de Julienne, Bruhl, Walpole, and Crozat collections, as well as the libraries of Voltaire and Diderot, she formed the basis of what is today the incredibly rich Hermitage Museum. Employing foreign and Russian architects, she built on an enormous scale with enthusiasm and taste, both public edifices and private dwellings for royal use.

Catherine as Grand Duchess, by G. C. Groot. (*The Russian Museum.*) Isolated from her husband, her children, and the Empress Elizabeth, she would often rise at three a.m. and ride for hours.

Catherine's generosity to her favorites is legendary; she gave a lifelong pension to Diderot and showered her lovers with titles, estates, palaces, and vast fortunes. She built the country palace of Gatchina and the Marble Palace in St. Petersburg for Grigori Orlov, whom she loved for twelve years and who gave her the world's fourth largest diamond for her scepter. For Potemkin she built the magnificent Tauride Palace, with a winter garden so large that it had a temple with her statue in the center, and thirty hothouse rooms filled with flowers, vegetables, and fruit trees. In 1791 Potemkin gave his fabled New Year's reception for Catherine there, one of the most extravagant evenings in the history of imperial Russia.

Catherine brought French civilization to the Russian court, replacing the Dutch and German influence that had preceded her. Where Peter the Great gave Russia a "window on Europe," Catherine the Great, mindful of his vision, established Russia as a great European power. She was succeeded by her son, Paul I.

On the 28th of June at six in the morning, Aleksey Orlov came into my room, woke me, and said, very calmly, "It is time for you to get up; everything is ready to proclaim you." I did not hesitate...I dressed as quickly as possible, without making a toilette, and I got into the carriage he had brought.... We got out [in Petersburg] at the barracks of the Ismaylovsky regiment.... The soldiers arrived, kissed me, embraced my feet, my hands, my clothes...two carried up a priest with a cross, and they began to take the oath.

After I resumed my seat in the carriage, the priest with the cross went in front of us and we went on to the Semenovsky [Regiment]. They came to meet us shouting "Vivat!" Now the procession, swollen by two regiments of the Guards, went with drums and Vivats!

I alighted at Kazan Cathedral. Then the Preobrazhensky Regiment arrived, also shouting "Vivat!" and saying "Forgive us for being the last to come, some of our officers tried to arrest us, but here are four of them whom we arrested, to show you our zeal. We want what our brothers want." The Horse Guards then came, led by their officers in such a frenzy of joy as I have never seen before, weeping and shouting that the country was free at last.... I went to the Winter Palace to take the measures necessary for success. There we had a consultation and it was resolved that I should go at the head of the army to Peterhof [where Peter III had been brought]....

After having despatched our couriers and taken all precautions, towards ten o'clock in the evening I dressed in guards' uniform.... So we rode through the night towards Peterhof.... Peter III renounced his empire, quite freely, surrounded by fifteen hundred Holsteiners. It was 29 June, St. Peter's Day, at noon.... Then the deposed emperor was taken twenty-seven versts from Peterhof, to Ropsha.... After two days of great fatigue they [the army] gave the order to leave at ten o'clock at night: provided, they said, that she comes with us. So I left with them; and half way, I rested in the country house of Kourakin, where I threw myself fully dressed on a bed. An officer pulled off my boots. I slept two-and-a-half hours. I mounted my horse again....

I went to mass; then they sang the Te Deum; then people came to congratulate me, me who since Friday at six in the morning had hardly drunk, eaten or slept. I was very glad to go to bed that Sunday night.

CATHERINE II, *Memoirs*

Tapestry: Countess Elizabeth Vorontsova (detail). Weaver: Jean Baptiste Rondet, St. Petersburg, 1762. (*The Metropolitan Museum of Art.*) Vorontsova was the mistress of Peter III; when he threatened to marry her and exile Catherine, Catherine overthrew him with the help of the Orlov brothers.

Opposite: Equestrian portrait of Catherine the Great at the time of her seizing of power, by Erichsen. (*Throne Room, Peterhof.*)

Right: Gold and enamel box with miniature of a gentleman, by J. P. Ador. St. Petersburg, eighteenth century. (*A La Vieille Russie.*)

Gentleman's court costume—satin with multi-colored embroidery. (*The Hermitage.*)

Right: Count Lvov. Dimitri Levitsky. (*The Russian Museum.*)

Left: Portrait of a Lady of the Grand Cross of the Order of Saint Catherine. (*The Metropolitan Museum of Art.*) The order consisted of two classes; the first was awarded to female members of the Imperial Family, the second to noblewomen and foreigners. There were only twelve Ladies of the Grand Cross and ninety-four of the Lesser Cross.

Question: *What Verb is conjugated most frequently of all at Court, and in what Tense?* Answer: *Even as at Court, so in the Capital, no one lives out of debt; therefore, the Verb conjugated most frequently of all is:* to be in debt. *(The appended Exemplary Conjugation is in the Present, since that is the Tense used most frequently of all.)*

> *I am in debt*
> *Thou art in debt*
> *He, She or It is in debt*
> *We are in debt*
> *You, Ye are in debt*
> *They are in debt*

Question: *Is this Verb ever conjugated in the Past Tense?* Answer: *Ever so rarely—inasmuch as no he or she pays his or her debts.* Q: *And in the Future Tense?* A: *The conjugation of this Verb in the Future Tense is in good usage, for it goes without saying that if one be not in debt yet, he or she inevitably* will be.

DENIS FONVIZIN. *Universal Courtier's Grammar,* 1783

Uniform of Field Marshal Suvorov—frock coat of green broadcloth embroidered with gold laurel leaves; waistcoat of red broadcloth. (*The Hermitage.*) (See page 24.)

Redingote: red velvet with white plush lining, gold buttons, gold braid buttonholes, 1790. (*The Hermitage.*)

Gentleman's court dress—frock coat, knee breeches, and embroidered satin waistcoat. (*The Hermitage.*)

Left: Duchesses E. N. Chovanskaya and E. N. Shrushtcheva in the roles of Lise and Colin. Dimitri Levitsky. (*The Russian Museum.*)

Silver soup tureen: part of a table service ordered by Catherine II for Prince Grigori Orlov. Jacques Nicolas Roettiers, Paris, 1770-1774. (*The Metropolitan Museum of Art.*)

Tea and coffee service, silver, parcel gilt with enamel medallions of Russian rulers. Johann Heinrich Blohm, St. Petersburg, 1773. (*The Metropolitan Museum of Art.*) Given by Catherine II to Count Peter Rumiantsev. In the war against the Turks (1769-1774), near Kagul, with an army of seventeen thousand, he defeated one hundred and fifty thousand Turks and was promoted to field marshal.

At Tsarskoe Selo there is going to be a terrible upheaval in the private apartments. The Empress has no desire to remain any longer in two unworthy rooms; she is going to pull down the main and only staircase at the end of the house; she wants to live in the midst of the three gardens; she wants to enjoy from her windows the same view as from the main balcony. She will have ten rooms, and for their decoration she will ransack her whole library and give her imagination free rein, and the result will be like these two pages: that is to say, quite without commonsense.

CATHERINE II, to Baron Grimm, 1778

Right: The Cameron Gallery at Tsarskoe Selo, 1784. Bashutzski, 1834.

The Orlov service totaled 3000 pieces. The inventories of only six shipments, from 1771 to 1773, account for 2,630 items, including:

576 dinner plates; 36 dozen sets of forks, knives, and spoons; 8 cruet frames; 128 assorted hors-d'oeuvres, second course, serving, and dessert plates; 8 braziers; 8 tureens with platters and serving forks; 8 *pots à oille* with platters and serving spoons; 36 saltcellars; 84 candlesticks; 8 mustard pots; 92 dish covers; 40 coffeepots ranging in size from two to twelve cups; 16 chocolate pots for two to ten cups; 24 five-branched candelabra; plus a variety of coffers, fish slicers, marrow spoons, wine coolers, sugar tongs, coffee spoons, snuffers, cream jugs, kettles, and sauceboats.

Catherine gave presents to reward, to buy loyalty, and to placate. She loved Orlov, but would never give him the one thing he wanted—the right to rule at her side. To appease him, she showered him with titles, estates, thousands of serfs, a suit covered with diamonds worth one million rubles, jeweled and enameled snuffboxes, miniatures, sword hilts, watches, precious Easter eggs, and the magnificent Sèvres Cameo Service now in the Hermitage.

Right: A soldier of the Cherson Infantry Regiment and an officer of the Poltava Infantry Regiment, 1776-1784. Viskovatov, 1844.

You cannot take towns by standing still.

CATHERINE II, proverb

Above and far right: Grenadiers with helmets, 1732-1756.

Everybody knows what the life of an army officer is like. In the morning, drilling and the riding-school; then dinner with the commander of the regiment, or at a Jewish tavern; in the evening, punch and cards. There was not one open house at ——, nor even one marriageable young lady; we used to gather in one another's rooms, where we never saw anything save our own uniforms.

ALEXANDER PUSHKIN, "The Shot"

Girandole: rock crystal, pink glass,
bronze, marble. Second half of the
eighteenth century. (*The Hermitage.*)

E. I. Nelidova, pupil at the Smolny
Institute. Dimitri Levitsky. (*Partridge
Room, Peterhof.*)

N. S. Borschtchova, pupil at the Smolny Institute. Dimitri Levitsky. (*The Russian Museum.*)

Woman's festival dress with a red brocade jacket, trimmed with gold; central Russia, late nineteenth century. (*The Historical Museum.*) Such elaborate holiday dresses belonged to the wives of rich peasant farmers. They were always worn with regional headdresses (see pages 130-133) and with jewelry of coral, pearls, and gold. The women could afford to have them made of such precious materials because they were handed down for generations and were shaped to fit a woman at any stage of life—youth, pregnancy, or old age.

Sarafan (traditional woman's festival garment) of Russian-manufactured brocade with gold lace front trim, over a tucked cotton blouse with jeweled woven gold necklace. (*The Historical Museum.*)

Left: Brocade of silver, gold, and many-colored silk threads. Attributed to Lazarev or Sapojnikov, eighteenth century, Moscow. (*The Metropolitan Museum of Art.*)

Stanislas Augustus Poniatowsky.

I am sending at once Count Kayserling as Ambassador to Poland to declare you King after the death of the present monarch.... I have twenty thousand precautions to take and have no time for harmful little love letters.

CATHERINE, to Stanislas Poniatowski

Do not make me a King! Only call me back to you!

PONIATOWSKI, to Catherine

Sergei Vassilievich Saltikov.

Unfortunately I could not help listening to him; he was as handsome as the dawn.... I held firm during the spring and part of the summer.

CATHERINE, on Sergei Saltikov

This one would have remained forever, had he not been the first to tire....

CATHERINE, on Grigori Orlov

Grigori Orlov.

Catherine II in the full dress of the Order of Saint Catherine.

If I may venture to be frank, I would say about myself that I was every inch a gentleman with a mind much more male than female; but together with this I was anything but masculine and combined, with the mind and temperament of a man, the attractions of a loveable woman.

CATHERINE, *A Frank Confession*

Ivan Rimsky-Korsakov.

The soul of Caesar and all the seductions of Cleopatra...

DENIS DIDEROT, on Catherine

You ask me if I am in love with him? Wonder and exaltation are called forth by this masterpiece of creation. He is the despair of painters, the unrealized dream of sculptors. He sends out warmth like the sun; he is the personification of every precious gift which nature in an orgy of prodigality has endowed a single human being....

CATHERINE, to Baron Grimm on Ivan Rimsky-Korsakov

Simon Zorich.

Snuffbox of translucent rose enamel over gold, with enamel portrait of Catherine II surrounded by thirty diamonds. Joseph Etienne Blerzy, Paris, c. 1775. (*The Metropolitan Museum of Art.*)

His Serene Highness, Grigori Alexandrovich Potemkin, Prince of Tauris.

Catherine had many terms of endearment for Potemkin:

My Cossack…heart of my heart…my golden pheasant…my peacock…dearest pigeon… wolf-bird…tiger…lion of the jungle…tomcat…my little heart…darling…dear…dearest doll…dear toy…my beauty…my marble beauty…my darling like no king on earth… I love you as I love my soul…I belong to you in every possible way…

CATHERINE, in letters to Potemkin

My pupil, my friend, my idol I must say, Prince Potemkin of Tauride has died.… His most beautiful characteristic was to me the greatness of his heart, his mind and his soul. Because of that we were always able to understand each other and ignore those who could not do so.… Whom can I rely on now?

CATHERINE, to Baron Grimm on the death of Potemkin

He will leap like a buck, and the color in his cheeks, which is always so beautiful, will grow brighter still, and his eyes, which shine like a pair of torches, will throw off sparks.

CATHERINE, to Baron Grimm on Alexander Lanskoy

A deep affliction has overwhelmed me and my whole happiness has fled. I thought that I should die after the irreparable loss of my best friend. I educated this young man; he was gentle, treatable, grateful, and I hoped he would be the support of my old age.... I have become a desperate, monosyllabic creature.... I cannot set eyes on a human face without tears choking my words.

CATHERINE, to Baron Grimm after Lanskoy's death

Alexander Dimitrievich Lanskoy.

Catherine II's bedroom at Peterhof. The L-shaped divan-bed on a dais runs the width of the room. The cover and pillows are of brocade—white, pale blue, and silver.

We are as clever as the very devil...we adore music...we hide our fondness for poetry as though it were a crime.

CATHERINE, to Baron Grimm on Alexander Dimitriev-Mamanov

Alexander Dmitriev-Mamanov.

78

Catherine II, by Alexander Roslin. (*A La Vieille Russie.*)

Alexander Petrovich Yermolov.

Platon Alexandrovich Zubov.

God is my judge that I did not take them (lovers) out of looseness, to which I have no inclination. If fate had given me in youth a husband whom I could have loved, I should have remained always true to him. The trouble is that my heart would not willingly remain one hour without love.

CATHERINE

Diamond fringe necklace, eighteenth century. (*A La Vieille Russie.*)

Woman's festival dress; rose silk *sarafan* with multi-colored embroidery and gold galloons and sash, over tambour-embroidered white batiste blouse. Central Russia, second half of the eighteenth century. (*The Historical Museum.*)

The Russian court retains many traces of its ancient Asiatic pomp, blended with European refinement. An immense retinue of courtiers always preceded and followed the empress; the costliness of their apparel, and a profusion of precious stones, created a splendour, of which the magnificence of other courts can give us only a faint idea.... Amid the several articles of sumptuousness which distinguish the Russian nobility there is none perhaps more calculated to strike a foreigner than the profusion of diamonds and other precious stones, which sparkle in every part of their dress.... The men vie with the fair sex in the use of them. Many of the nobility were almost covered with diamonds.

ARCHDEACON COXE, 1784

Snuffbox of gold and opalescent enamel, decorated with rosettes and pearls, with the cipher of Catherine II set in diamonds. Jean Joseph Barrière, Paris, c. 1782. (*The Metropolitan Museum of Art.*)

Right: Coronation dress of Catherine II embroidered with the Romanov double-headed eagle. (*The Kremlin Armory.*)

Equestrian Statue of Peter the Great by E.-M. Falconet. Drawing by
B. Patersen, 1805. Commissioned by Catherine, the statue took twelve
years to complete. She had inscribed on the base: "Petro Primo Cath-
arina Secunda."

To introduce Russian dress at court, Catherine issued ukases stating when it
should be worn. Here she wears a modified version of the *kokochnik*, the traditional Russian headdress. Her adaptation of Russian elements is best seen in her
"dress uniforms" (page 17). Catherine was Honorary Colonel of many army and
marine regiments. When she appeared before them on special occasions—a military review, the launching of a ship—she wore a peculiar costume of her own
invention, in the colors of the dress uniform of the regiment, decorated with regu-
lation galloons and buttons. The shape is French, a wide dress mounted on a
farthingale. The placement of the gold decoration is similar to that on the richly
brocaded festival dresses worn by wealthy farmers' wives (pages 73, 80, 136, 138)
and on the field caftan of Peter I (page 32).

Portrait of Catherine II in Russian Dress. Erichsen.

If this war continues, my garden at Tsarskoe will look like a skittle alley, for at each brilliant stroke, I have a monument erected.

CATHERINE, to Voltaire

In spite of everything, I am as eager as a five-year-old to play blindman's bluff, and the young people, my grandchildren and great-grandchildren say that their games are never so merry as when I am there.

CATHERINE

If I could live to be a hundred, I would wish to unite the whole of Europe under the scepter of Russia. But I have no intention of dying before I have driven the Turks out of Constantinople, broken the pride of the Chinese and established commerce with India.

CATHERINE

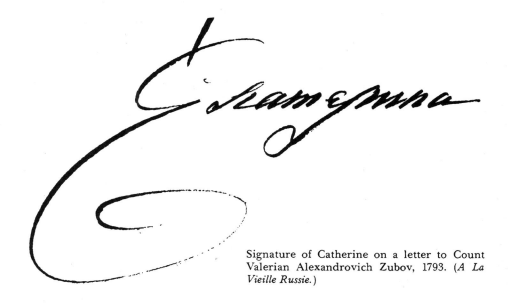

Signature of Catherine on a letter to Count Valerian Alexandrovich Zubov, 1793. (*A La Vieille Russie.*)

Here lies
Catherine the Second
Born in Stettin on April 21, 1729.
She went to Russia in 1744 to marry Peter III. At the age of fourteen she made the threefold resolution to please her husband, Elizabeth, and the nation. She neglected nothing in trying to achieve this. Eighteen years of tedium and loneliness gave her the opportunity to read many books.

On the throne of Russia she wanted to do what was good for her country and tried to bring happiness, liberty and prosperity to her subjects.

She forgave easily and hated no one. She was tolerant, understanding and of happy disposition. She had a republican spirit and a kind heart.
She was sociable by nature.
She made many friends.
She took pleasure in her work.
She loved the arts.

CATHERINE—her epitaph, written by her four years before her death

Left: Catherine II with her favorite English whippet in the park at Tsarskoe Selo.

Box of silver gilt, niello, and *verre eglomisé*, with portrait of Paul I, c. 1800. (*The Metropolitan Museum of Art.*)

PAUL I

1796-1801

Born in 1754, the son of Catherine the Great was intensely disliked by his mother, who several times tried to remove him from the succession. Her coup against his father, Peter III, was a shock from which he never recovered, and he lived in constant fear of his own life. When he became Emperor, he made every effort to undo all that Catherine had done. He introduced a law of succession to strengthen the throne against the nobility; he dismissed Catherine's servants, refused to use her palaces, and replaced French influence with Prussian. He rescinded the rights of the nobles, limited the power of the Imperial Guards, and attempted to limit the exploitation of the serfs by the nobility. But his behavior was erratic, and his whimsical application of petty regulations caused great discontent. He seemed to be happiest drilling his soldiers at Gatchina or Pavlosk, but if one of them missed a step, the Emperor would cane him.

Paul was obsessed by fear of the French Revolution and went to extremes to keep it from "infecting" Russia; he forbade women to wear dresses cut in the latest French styles, and prevented Russians from traveling to foreign countries and from importing Western books and music.

In 1798 Paul joined the second coalition against France, but withdrew from it and formed a league with Prussia, Sweden, and Denmark to counter English interference in neutral shipping. He also ordered an abortive invasion of India.

Paul was married to the devoted Sophia of Württemberg (Maria Feodorovna); they had seven children, two of whom eventually became Emperors, Alexander I and Nicholas

Pavlosk: the Pilaster Room by Giacomo Quarenghi.

I. Toward the end of his reign he attempted to violate his own law of succession and placed the Tsarevich Alexander under house arrest, threatening to give the throne to his wife's German nephew. His insane behavior led to a guards' conspiracy to force his abdication. He refused to resign, and the conspirators strangled him on the night of March 23, 1801, in the heavily guarded Mikhailovsky Castle. His son and successor, Alexander I, knew of the conspiracy but did not participate in the murder.

In the temple is an octagonal altar, of amber and ivory; on the central face are my initials...on the other faces are those of my seven children, beginning with Alexander...and ending with the late dear Olinka. I had made this gift last year to the dear Grand Duke when dear Olinka was still alive and when Annette was not yet born. I have painted all the ciphers of the children in roses and myrtle; mine is in little blue flowers. Above the altar is a little bronze statue with the attributes of conjugal and filial love.

MARIA FEODOROVNA, 1795

Miniature of Alexander I. Ange-
lique Zeller. (*A La Vieille Russie.*)

ALEXANDER I

1801-1825

Born in 1777, Alexander was taken at birth from his parents and raised by his grandmother, Catherine II, to be her successor. Influenced in his youth by his liberal tutor, Frédéric César de la Harpe, and by the rigid military discipline of his favorite, Alexei Arakcheev, Alexander vacillated all his life between liberal and despotic policies.

He introduced reforms early in his reign and tried to forge alliances that would lead to a European federation, but this was frustrated by the rise of Napoleon I. When Alexander met Napoleon on the raft at Tilsit, he pretended to acquiesce in Napoleon's long-range plans for Europe, in order to gain time. When Napoleon invaded Russia in 1812, Alexander was forced to give supreme command of the armies to sixty-seven-year-old Prince Mikhail Kutuzov, whom he despised. Declining to sue for peace, Alexander saw Napoleon's Grand Army of six hundred thousand troops reduced to thirty thousand in the disastrous retreat from Moscow. He was then able to enter Paris in triumph and to participate in negotiations to restore peace in Europe, at the same time gaining control of Poland, of which he made himself King.

Alexander had been married at the age of sixteen to Princess Marie Louise of Baden, then fourteen, but their childless marriage was an unhappy one. Later in life, he came under the influence of the pietistic visionary Barbara Juliane von Krudener. He formed the Holy Alliance with Austria and Prussia, which was idealistic in intent but became a symbol of monarchial despotism. During his reign, the leading writers were Krylov and Pushkin. After his death, when he was succeeded by his brother Nicholas I, a legend arose that Alexander was living in Siberia as a pious recluse.

Right: The Empress Elizabeth Alexeevna (formerly Princess Marie Louise of Baden), wife of Alexander I.

Ball gown: tulle, embroidered with steel plaquettes from Tula, c. 1820. (*The Hermitage.*) (See page 22.)

Box of gold and enamel. K.-C. Kanz, St. Petersburg, c. 1820. (*The Metropolitan Museum of Art.*)

The riches of Kaïb were inexhaustible; his palace, one historian informs us, was girt about with a thousand pillars of jasper, the capitals thereof being of solid emerald, and of the Corinthian order, while their bases were of refined gold; the palace itself was builded of black marble, and its walls were so smoothly polished that the daintiest damsels regarded themselves therein as if in a mirror. The proportions of the windows were those of the latest Italian architecture — constructed only just a trifle bigger than the gates of a city — and each window was set with but a single pane, yet so strong was the glass that the most brazen-browed yea-saying men of our time would have found it beyond them to break a hole therein with their foreheads. The roof was of sheet silver, but so trimly worked that often, on clear days, the whole city would come running to the palace thinking it on fire, whereas all the alarum had been created solely by the glitter of the roof.

I. A. KRYLOV's satire, *Kaïb*

Above: Alexander I visiting the English portrait painter George Dawe in his studio in the Winter Palace. Dawe painted nearly all the portraits in the Winter Palace Military Hall, of the generals who fought against Napoleon.

Cashmere dress with embroidered flounces; red shawl with double-faced woven floral border, c. 1820. (*The Hermitage.*)

Shawls like this could cost a hundred thousand gold rubles, the price of a thousand serfs. They were worn summer and winter, even at balls. Made from the fleeces of Tibetan goats and Saiga antelopes, they were woven in double-faced technique, so that both sides were indistinguishable. Some took three years to make, and were woven by female serfs on the estates of landed noblewomen. The young girls who wove them often went blind and were then retired to special homes.

Stroganov Palace and Police Bridge, on the Nevsky Prospect
and Moika Canal, St. Petersburg. B. Patersen, 1799.

A really extraordinary idea, to put the capital of Russia at the world's end!... As though Moscow were not cold enough, we had to be given Petersburg! And the wild wasteland that separates Mother Moscow from her little son! The air is heavy with fog and the wan, grey-green earth bears nothing except charred tree-stumps, pines and hummocks of grass.... The only consolation is the dead-straight road along which the singing, rattling troikas carry one at lightning speed. And what a difference, what a tremendous difference, between the two towns!

Even today Moscow is still the bearded Russian, while Petersburg is already a polished European. Old Moscow spreads itself out and lolls at ease, whereas Petersburg, the fop, stands at attention, fingers pressed against trouser-seams! Mirrors surround it on all sides—the Neva, the Gulf of Finland, the canals. Ample opportunity for self-admiration...Petersburg is in perpetual motion, from cellar to attic; at midnight it begins to bake the French rolls which will be devoured next morning by all the different nationalities that make up its population, and one or another of its yellow eyes is always blinking through the darkness. Whereas Moscow snores all night and sets out at daybreak, crossing itself and bowing to all four points of the compass, to eat its modest breakfast in the market.

Petersburg is a gentleman of scrupulous deportment, a true German, reck-
oning every penny and carefully weighing his purse before sending out invitations
for a soirée; but Moscow is a grand seigneur, pursuing a pleasure, once begun,
to the point of exhaustion, with little care for the fact that his funds have long given
out....

The Moscow newspapers speak of Kant, Schelling and so forth; the Petersburg papers talk of nothing but the public and solvency. In Moscow the papers keep
pace with the times, but are apt to be late in appearing; in Petersburg the papers
are entirely behind the times, but appear punctually at the appointed hour. In Moscow a writer can whistle for his money, in Petersburg he earns some.

Moscow, swathed in bearskins, drives in carriages, usually on the way to a
meal; Petersburg, hands in mackintosh pockets, rushes on foot to the Stock Ex-
change or "to go on duty." The whole of Russia glides in sledges to Moscow in the
winter, to buy and sell; the peasants trudge to Petersburg in the summer, to find
work. Moscow is a huge warehouse, Petersburg a brightly-lit shop. Moscow is indispensable to Russia, Russia is indispensable to Petersburg....

Petersburg is fond of laughing at Moscow for its bad taste and awkwardness,
but Moscow retorts scornfully that Petersburg cannot even speak Russian.

NIKOLAI GOGOL, "St. Petersburg," *Notes of 1836*

Pavlosk Palace and park. A. Martynov, 1822.

Alexander I's day:

At 6 a.m. he took tea, and after dressing went into the park where the gardener, Liamine, waited — also swans, ducks and geese who, seeing him in the distance, gave loud cries. The Emperor fed them, gave his orders to the gardener, and continued his walk. At 10 a.m. he got back, and sometimes ate fruit.... About that time Liamine brought fruit picked in the orangeries, and the Emperor sent it to those of the Court who were staying in the Chinese Village. Then he changed his clothes, and received his ministers and the Chief of the General Staff. At 3 p.m. he went to Pavlovsk to see his mother. At 4 p.m. he dined; and after tea at 9 p.m. he worked in his study. At 11 p.m. he took curds or plums, and went to bed, when he fell into a profound sleep.

Les Trésors d'Art en Russie, 1904

Ball gown of white batiste with embroidery, c. 1810. (*The Hermitage.*)

Natasha was going to her first grand ball. She had got up at eight that morning and had been in a fever of excitement and activity all day.... The countess was to wear a claret-colored velvet dress, and the two girls white gauze over pink silk slips, with roses on their bodices and their hair dressed à la grecque....

In the damp chill air and crowded closeness of the swaying carriage, she for the first time vividly imagined what was in store for her there at the ball, in those brightly lighted rooms — with music, flowers, dances, the Emperor, and all the brilliant young people of Petersburg.... She understood all that awaited her only when...she ...mounted the brightly illuminated stairs between the flowers. Only then did she remember how she must behave at a ball, and tried to assume the majestic air she considered indispensable for a girl on such an occasion.... Before and behind them other visitors were entering, also talking in low tones and wearing ball dresses. The mirrors on the landing reflected ladies in white, pale-blue, and pink dresses, with diamonds and pearls on their bare necks and arms....

She was not concerned about the Emperor...she had but one thought: "Is it possible no one will ask me, that I shall not be among the first to dance?... They must know how I long to dance, how splendidly I dance, and how they would enjoy dancing with me."...

Prince Andrew, in the white uniform of a cavalry colonel, wearing stockings and dancing shoes,...recognized her, guessed her feelings, saw that it was her debut.... He asked her to waltz....

"I have long been waiting for you," that frightened happy little girl seemed to say by the smile that replaced the threatened tears, as she raised her hand to Prince Andrew's shoulder.

LEO TOLSTOY, *War and Peace*

Malachite vase, nine feet two inches high, on a bronze pedestal with gilt-bronze ornaments, by Pierre Philippe Thomire, Paris, 1819. It was commissioned by Count Nicholas Demidov, Russian Ambassador to Florence, whose family, enriched under Peter I, owned vast malachite mines in the Urals. At the time of the Demidov sale in 1880, this vase was described as supporting a gilt-bronze candelabra of nineteen branches. (*The Metropolitan Museum of Art.*)

The Winter Palace, 1825.

In the Summer evenings...the citizens of Petersburg delight in sailing upon the Neva in their pleasure boats. The boats of the nobility are very elegantly ornamented. The company are seated in the stern, under a canopy of silk or other stuff, and have with them musicians, or frequently the party themselves perform upon different instruments. The rowers are all chosen from among such of their servants as have the best voices.... When they have rowed their boat against the stream,...they allow her to drive with the current,

...and the rowers collect in a circle. They...make such exquisite harmony as to draw the inhabitants to the galleries of their houses upon the river's banks, and the foot passengers to the water's edge, to listen to the music; and many follow the boat, to enjoy their native tunes.... When the concert is ended, the audience upon the streets goes away, repeating the songs, and echoing them into every quarter of the city....

ANDREW SWINTON, *Travels*, 1792

Plate: Imperial Manufacture, St. Petersburg, 1801-1825. In the center, a medallion encloses a view of the Church of St. John the Baptist, Florence. Part of a service painted with views of Italy which was presented by Alexander I to his sister, Queen Catherine of Württemberg. (*The Metropolitan Museum of Art.*)

The two princes Alexander Pavlovich...aged 4 years. Constantine Pavlovich...aged 3 years. They are beautiful and sensible and clever. Empress allows 30,000 rubles a year for their clothes. We went for a walk with them in the garden, two Englishwomen who have charge of them are sisters. Mrs Guslar and Mrs Nichols, both civil. Empress ordered them to call [the princes] by their christian names only, as pride would come fast enough without encouraging it.... Empress is very fond of them and cannot refuse them anything, nothing pleases them like soldiers and exercising. Each of them would have a regiment, twenty-four boys, two in turn to guard their apartments. Prince Alexander knows all the uniforms of the Empress's services, as much as the officers.

ELIZABETH DIMSDALE, unpublished diary, 1781 (quoted in Kennett)

Left: Kamennostrovsky Palace. Alexander I and his commander-in-chief, Prince Kutuzov, met here in 1812 to plan the offensive against Napoleon.

Tsarevich Alexander (sitting on the ground), among his cadets at Peterhof. The cadet corps were important for military training of the nobility.

Moscow burning, as Napoleon's cavalry enters the Kremlin, September 2, 1812.

Such terrible tactics have no precedent in the history of civilization.... To burn one's own cities!... A demon inspires these people! What savage determination! What a people! What a people!

NAPOLEON, September 1812

You fear a retreat through Moscow, but I regard it as far-sighted, because it will save the army. Napoleon is like a stormy torrent which we are as yet unable to stop. Moscow will be the sponge that will suck him in.

M. I. KUTUZOV,
Field Marshal, 1812

Courier with three horses. G. Orlovski, 1825.

Tribesman Wearing Turban and
Plumes. J.-B. Le Prince, 1768.

Balaga was a famous troyka driver.... More than once when Anatole's regiment was stationed at Tver he had taken him from Tver in the evening, brought him to Moscow by daybreak, and driven him back again the next night. More than once he had enabled Dolokhov to escape when pursued. More than once he had driven them through the town with gypsies and "ladykins" as he called the cocottes. More than once in their service he had run over pedestrians and upset vehicles in the streets of Moscow and had always been protected from the consequences by "my gentlemen" as he called them. He had ruined more than one horse in their service. More than once they had beaten him, and more than once they had made him drunk on champagne and Madeira, which he loved; and he knew more than one thing about each of them which would long ago have sent an ordinary man to Siberia. They often called Balaga into their orgies and made him drink and dance at the gypsies', and more than one thousand rubles of their money had passed through his hands. In their service he risked his skin and his life twenty times a year, and in their service had lost more horses than the money he had from them would buy. But he liked them; liked that mad driving at twelve miles an hour, liked upsetting a driver or running down a pedestrian, and flying at full gallop through the Moscow streets. He liked to hear those wild, tipsy shouts behind him: "Get on! Get on!" when it was impossible to go any faster. He liked giving a painful lash on the neck to some peasant who, more dead than alive, was already hurrying out of his way. "Real gentlemen!" he considered them.

LEO TOLSTOY, *War and Peace*

Troika, St. Petersburg, 1824.

A merchant's wife from Kaluga, 1804.

...a new diversion we have had at court this winter. There is a machine made of boards, that goes from the upper story down to the yard; it is broad enough for a coach, with a little ledge on each side. This had water flung upon it, which soon froze, and then more was flung, till it was covered with ice of a considerable thickness. The ladies and gentlemen of the court sit on sledges, and they are set going at the top, and fly down to the bottom; for the motion is so swift, that nothing but flying is a proper term. Sometimes, if these sledges meet with any resistance, the person in them tumbles head over heels; that, I suppose, is the joke.... I was terrified out of my wits for fear of being obliged to go down this shocking place, for I had not only the dread of breaking my neck, but of being exposed to indecency too frightful to think on without horror.

MRS. WARD, wife of a diplomat, 1735

Left: Ice Hill at Tobolsk. Rechberg, 1810.

Right: A married woman from Waldai, 1804.

The arrival of a rich neighbor marks a great epoch for those who live in the country. The landowners and their house serfs discuss the matter for two months before the arrival and for three years afterward.

ALEXANDER PUSHKIN, "The Shot"

Peasants Dancing. Houbigant, *Moeurs et Costumes,* 1821.

Carriage on sleigh runners with liveried attendants. J. A. Atkinson, 1803.

...coats trimmed with furs so expensive foreigners are astonished.... These coats, of very fine material, are lined with sable or musk and have collars made out of beaver costing from one hundred to three hundred roubles, depending on whether the pelt is thicker, softer, or darker in color and on the number of white hairs sticking out. A coat worth a thousand roubles is not considered exorbitant, there are some worth much more;...in Saint Petersburg one could make a [proverb]: "Tell me what furs you wear, and I will tell you how much you are worth." One is judged according to one's furs.

THEOPHILE GAUTIER, *Voyage en Russie*, 1865

Left: Embroidered linen edged with bobbin lace, nineteenth century. (*The Metropolitan Museum of Art.*)

A Russian Gentlewoman in Winter Traveling Costume. Atkinson, 1803.

Officer of the Special Caucasus Corps, Cossack Regiment. (*The Metropolitan Museum of Art.*)

A Tatar Girl. Rechberg. *Peuples de la Russie*, 1810.

Occasionally one sees an officer on horseback galloping at a great pace to take an order to some troop commander; sometimes it is a courier who is "taking the order" to some provincial governor, perhaps at the other end of the Empire.... Farther off, some infantrymen are coming back from drill and presenting themselves at their quarters to take orders from their captain—nothing but superior officers who command inferior officers.... One does not die, one does not breathe here except by permission or by imperial order; therefore, everything is gloomy and constrained.... Officers, coachmen, Cossacks, serfs, courtiers, all are servants, of different rank, of the same master and blindly obeying an idea that they do not understand. It is a masterpiece of military mechanics; but the sight of this beautiful order does not satisfy me at all, as so much regularity cannot be obtained except through the complete absence of independence. I seem to see the shadow of death hovering over this part of the globe.

MARQUIS DE CUSTINE, *Lettres de Russie*, 1839

Right: A Khan of the Crimea. G. Orlovski, 1819.

He is stern and severe — *with fixed principles of* duty *which* nothing *on earth will make him change: very* clever *I do* not *think him.*

QUEEN VICTORIA, on Nicholas I, 1844

Gold medal depicting Nicholas I, 1859. (*A La Vieille Russie.*)

NICHOLAS I

1825-1855

The third son of Paul I, nineteen years younger than his brother Emperor Alexander I, Nicholas was born in 1796. He profited little from his extensive education, being interested primarily in the army. At the time of his accession to the throne, the political situation was precarious. His older brother Constantine had secretly renounced the throne and married a Polish noblewoman, but Nicholas, not wanting to seem eager for power, swore allegiance to Constantine. Out of this combination of secrecy and confusion came the Decembrist Conspiracy. The Decembrists were primarily noblemen, many of them officers, who had accompanied the Emperor Alexander I to Paris on his triumphal tour after the Napoleonic war. There they had breathed the freedom in the air of France and had witnessed the openness of French society. On December 26, 1825, three thousand of these misled rebels marched to the Senate Square, starting a disastrous mutiny. Nicholas, with great reluctance, was forced to fire on them, thus ascending the throne over the bodies of his subjects. He never recovered from this shock, which affected his entire reign. Even though some of the Decembrists had been his close friends, he mercilessly exiled them with their families to Siberia for the rest of their lives. Years later he would not hear of mercy, even for their wives.

Nicholas' rule was characterized by his remark, "I cannot permit that any individual should defy my wishes, once he knows what they are." But his severity was based on fear, not on self-confidence. Throughout his life, he was unsure of himself and could never tolerate the slightest frustration. His regime was one of militarism and bureaucracy and he prevented reform of almost any kind.

As an admirer of all things Prussian, especially the army, he gave obsessive attention to uniforms, designing hundreds of them for everyone from generals to school children. One of the three rulers (along with Peter I and Catherine II) to issue ukases on civil dress, he decreed in 1834 that the *kokochnik* with tulle veil attached should be worn by ladies-in-waiting at court ceremonies. His censorship, secret police, and persecution of liberals all contributed to the revolutionary movement. During his regime, two great schools of thought—Slavophile and Western—emerged, and with the writings of Pushkin, Lermontov, and Gogol a golden age in literature began.

Nicholas was known as the most handsome monarch in Europe. He married Princess Charlotte of Prussia (Empress Alexandra Feodorovna), with whom he had six children. Nicholas' reign ended in the disaster of the Crimean War, where because of his miscalculations he found himself alone fighting the Ottoman Empire, England, France, and Sardinia. He was succeeded by his son, Alexander II.

Empress Alexandra Feodorovna, daughter of Frederick William III of Prussia, wife of Nicholas I. Lithograph by Maurin from a painting by Christina Robertson.

The Tsarina is a most elegant figure in spite of her extreme thinness... her eyes... betrayed profound suffering borne with angelic calm.... She has given too many idols to Russia, too many children to the Emperor.... Everyone sees the Tsarina's condition: no one speaks of it.... Is she feverish?... The Emperor nurses her...but as soon as she recovers he kills her again with activity, feasts, voyages, love...in Russia all must follow the Imperial whirlwind, smiling until death.

MARQUIS DE CUSTINE, 1839

Submission in Russia makes you believe there is uniformity; correct this idea. Nowhere is there a country where there is such diversity of races, of customs, of religion, or mentality as in Russia. The differences are basic; the uniformity superficial, and unity is only apparent. There near us you see twenty officers: only the first two are Russians; the next three are reconciled Poles; some of the others are German; there is everything, even to Kirghiz khans who bring me their sons to be reared among my cadets. There is one of them.

Two hundred thousand children are reared and instructed along with this child at my expense.

NICHOLAS I, to the Marquis de Custine, 1839

Above and at far left: Life Guards, Circassian Squadron. (*The Metropolitan Museum of Art.*)

Center: Proclamation of the Coronation of Nicholas I in Red Square, Moscow. Lithograph by Courtin, 1826.

Top: Kuban Cossacks, Special Caucasus Corps. (*The Metropolitan Museum of Art.*)

Bottom: Don Cossacks, Special Caucasus Corps. (*The Metropolitan Museum of Art.*)

Candleholder (right) and razor (below). Johann Bernhard Hertz, St. Petersburg, c. 1848. From a gentleman's traveling case containing forty-five pieces, made for Ralph Isaacs Ingersoll, Minister Plenipotentiary from President Polk to the Court of Alexander II. Among other silver, crystal, ivory, and gold pieces in the silk-lined case are two engraved basins, a pitcher with an ivory handle, a covered shaving cup, a tub for a shaving stick, a shaving brush, a container for matches, four silver-topped crystal boxes, a crystal bottle, an ink bottle, a pounce shaker, a pen handle, a pencil, a seal, a letter opener, a penknife, a corkscrew, four razors with ivory handles, mustache scissors, nail scissors, a nail file, tweezers and an earspoon, a stiletto, a buttonhook, a hat brush, a hair brush, a comb for hair, and a comb for lice. (*The Metropolitan Museum of Art.*)

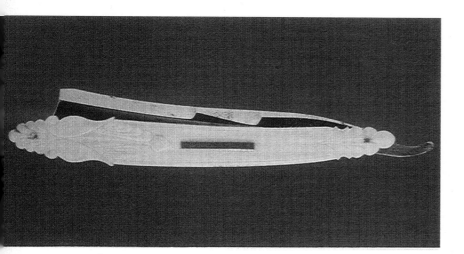

Amber on Tsargrad's pipes,
porcelain and bronzes on a table,
and — of the pampered senses joy —
perfumes in crystal cut with facets;
combs, little files of steel,
straight scissors, curvate ones,
and brushes of thirty kinds —
these for the nails, those for the teeth.
Rousseau (I shall observe in passing)
could not understand how dignified Grimm
dared clean his nails in front of him,
the eloquent crackbrain.
The advocate of liberty and rights
was in the present case not right at all.

ALEXANDER PUSHKIN, *Eugene Onegin*

The evening before Oblomov had received a disagreeable letter from the bailiff of his estate:... bad harvest, debts, smaller income, etc. Although the bailiff had written exactly the same letter the year before and the year before that, his last letter had the effect of an unpleasant surprise.

It was no joke! One had to think of taking some measures. In justice to Ilya Ilyitch it must be said that, after receiving the bailiff's first unpleasant letter several years before, he had begun to think of various changes and improvements in the management of his estate.... But the plan was not yet thoroughly thought out, and the bailiff's unpleasant letters came every year inciting him to action and disturbing his peace of mind. Oblomov knew it was necessary to do something decisive.

As soon as he woke he made up his mind to get up and wash, and, after drinking tea, to think matters over, taking various things into consideration and writing them down, and altogether to go into the subject thoroughly. He lay for half an hour tormented by his decision; but afterwards he reflected that he would have time to think after breakfast, which he could have in bed as usual, especially since one can think just as well lying down.

IVAN GONCHAROV, *Oblomov*, 1859

Left: The Aristocrat's Breakfast. P. A. Fedotov, 1849. Impoverished by gambling, this young nobleman hides his crust of bread as he hears a visitor coming. (*The Tretyakov Museum.*)

Right: Military Gallery in the Winter Palace; the portrait at the far end is of Alexander I. In the foreground: left, Wellington; right, Kutuzov. Most of the portraits were painted by George Dawe. Drawing by Sadovnikov.

General's uniform, the Terek Cossack Guards (the Tsar's own convoy), 1860. (*The Hermitage.*)

Right: Porcelain vase with portrait of Frederick William III of Prussia. Russian Imperial Porcelain Factory. (*A La Vieille Russie.*)

Cossack uniform, Winter Palace livery, late nineteenth century. (*The Hermitage.*)

They were playing cards with Namurov of the Horse Guards. The long winter night slipped by imperceptibly; it was five in the morning when they broke off to eat. Those who had won ate with a hearty appetite; the others stared abstractedly at empty plates. But champagne appeared; the talk became livelier, and soon everyone joined in.

ALEXANDER PUSHKIN,
The Queen of Spades

Parade in the Winter Palace Square, St. Petersburg. Perrot.

Below: The Order of Saint Andrew: gold and enamel badge, collar, sash, and silver star. Keibel, mid-nineteenth century. (*A La Vieille Russie*.) Founded in 1698 by Peter the Great, this is the oldest order of the Russian Empire.

Top and bottom: Chessmen: silver, silver-gilt, with precious stones, nineteenth century. (*The Metropolitan Museum of Art.*)

Portrait of Evgraf Davydov. Orest Kiprensky, 1809. (*The Russian Museum.*) A colonel of the Hussar Regiment in the Imperial Guard, Davydov was the prototype of the chivalrous, nonchalant young officers of democratic spirit who emerged from the Napoleonic War. Tolstoy used him as the model for Vaska Denisov in *War and Peace*.

Up to the entrance hall our hero now has driven;
past the concierge he, like an arrow,
has flown up the marble stairs,
has run his fingers through his hair,
has entered. The ballroom is full of people;
the music has already tired of crashing;
the crowd is occupied with the mazurka;
there's all around both noise and crush;
there clink the cavalier guard's spurs;
the little feet of winsome ladies flit;
upon their captivating tracks
flit flaming glances,
and by the roar of violins is drowned
the jealous whispering of fashionable women.

ALEXANDER PUSHKIN, *Eugene Onegin*

Ball gown, white silk tulle, white embroidery sewn with brilliants, lantern sleeves; worn with flat dancing slippers, 1830. (*The Hermitage.*)

One must be Russian and even Tsar to stand up under the fatigue of life in Petersburg at this moment: in the evening, fêtes such as one sees only in Russia; in the morning, court felicitations, ceremonies, receptions, or perhaps public solemnities, parades on land and sea—for example, a vessel of 120 cannons launched on the Neva in the presence of the court re-enforced by the entire city. Such are the things that absorb my energy and engage my curiosity.

MARQUIS DE CUSTINE, 1839

General's uniform, Life Guard Hussar regiment. The short jacket was worn on the left shoulder to free the right arm for using the saber. 1825-1855. (*The Hermitage.*) The poet Lermontov was dishonorably discharged from this regiment for his poem on the death of Pushkin.

Left: The Jordan Staircase, Winter Palace. Sadovnikov. The Tsar descended this staircase each year on January 6 for the ceremony of the Baptism of the Neva.

"Well, bonne chance," she added, giving Vronsky a finger
that was not engaged in holding her fan, and with a shrug of
her shoulders making the bodice of her dress, which had ridden up a little, slip down again that she might be befittingly
naked when she moved forward to the front of her box and
into the glare of gas-light and the gaze of all eyes.

LEO TOLSTOY, *Anna Karenin*

Batiste morning dress with crinoline, c. 1860. (*The Hermitage.*)

Right: Embroidered dress of white moiré with bustle
and train, 1870. (*The Historical Museum.*)

Fan with embossed gold paper decoration, and sticks of ivory, the guard ornamented with mother-of-pearl and inlaid with Bulgarian silver, nineteenth century. (*The Metropolitan Museum of Art.*)

Tatiana believed in the lore
of plain-folk ancientry,
dreams, cartomancy,
and the predictions of the moon.
Portents disturbed her:
mysteriously all objects
foretold her something,
presentiments constrained her breast.
The mannered tomcat sitting on the stove,
purring, might wash his muzzlet with his paw:
to her 'twas an indubitable sign
that guests were coming. Seeing all at once
the young two-horned moon's visage
in the sky on her left…

ALEXANDER PUSHKIN, *Eugene Onegin*

Princess Tcherkassaya. P. Soklov, 1847. (*The Russian Museum.*)

Family Portrait. Feodor Tolstoy, 1830. (*The Russian Museum.*)

Merchants, who form a middle class, are so few in number that they have no influence on the state. Writers can be counted one or two to each generation. Artists are like writers; the smallness of their number causes them to be esteemed: but while their rarity enhances their personal fortune, it detracts from their social influence. There are no lawyers in a country where there is no justice.

MARQUIS DE CUSTINE, 1839

Left: Albrecht, Major General in Retirement.
Orest Kiprensky, 1827. (*The Russian Museum.*)

The Emperor at Rest. Nicholas I on a hunting trip in the Tyrol; colored lithograph, c. 1835. (*A La Vieille Russie.*)

Right: Pagoda-style dress of white muslin, printed with the cucumber motif; worn over crinoline; sleeve and skirt flounces trimmed with lace, 1850. (*The Historical Museum.*)

Blue glass transfer-decorated beakers. Imperial Porcelain Factory, c. 1840. (*A La Vieille Russie.*)

Porcelain vase, mauve and gilt. Imperial Porcelain Factory, 1829. (*A La Vieille Russie.*)

The Winter Palace, 1825.

I saw the façade of the new Winter Palace.... In one year this palace rose up out of its ashes....

In order to finish the work in the period specified by the Emperor, unprecedented efforts were required. The interior construction was continued during the bitterest cold of winter. Six thousand laborers were continually at work; a considerable number died each day, but, as the victims were instantly replaced by other champions who filled their places, to perish in their turn in this inglorious gap, the losses were not apparent.

During freezes of fifteen to twenty degrees below zero, six thousand obscure martyrs ...were shut up in rooms heated to eighty-six degrees in order to dry the walls more

quickly. Thus these wretches on entering and leaving this abode of death...underwent a difference in temperature of 100 to 108 degrees....

I have been told that the unfortunate ones who painted the interior of the hottest rooms were obliged to put a kind of ice cap on their heads in order to keep their senses under the boiling temperature they were condemned to endure while they were working....

Nevertheless, the sovereign was called "Father" by men sacrificed in such great numbers under his eyes.

MARQUIS DE CUSTINE, 1839

Above and right: Two paintings of women's festival headdresses, late nineteenth century. (*The Historical Museum.*)

Left and far right: Four peasant headdresses of the 1830s. Solntzev, 1869.

The headdress, or *kokochnik*, differed in each region. In the north they were heavily embroidered with gold thread and river seed pearls, with a pearl net descending over the forehead. In the central regions they were tall, those from Vladimir and Nizhni Novgorod crescent-shaped, those of Kostroma peaked. In the south they were the most complicated; those of Ryazan and Tamakov were called *sosoki* (magpies), and had horns and long red streamers. In Voronezh and Kursk they were decorated with strips of multicolored embroidery.

The married woman wore a covered headdress; according to ancient Slavic custom, she had to hide her hair from the eyes of strangers. The maiden wore a hoop which revealed her hair in back, plaited into a single braid. During the wedding, the bride changed headdresses, and this ritual was accompanied by special chants and lamentations.

Four paintings of women's festival headdresses (far right: a bride), late nineteenth century. (*The Historical Museum.*)

Still amors, devils, serpents
on the stage caper and make noise;
still the tired footmen
sleep on the pelisses at the carriage porch;
still people have not ceased to stamp,
blow noses, cough, hiss, clap;
still, outside and inside,
lanterns shine everywhere;
still, feeling chilled, the horses fidget,
bored with their harness,
and the coachmen around the fires
curse their masters and beat their palms together;
and yet Onegin has already left;
he's driving home to dress.

ALEXANDER PUSHKIN, *Eugene Onegin*

Satin dress with lace shawl, made by serfs of the landed gentry, 1850. (*The Hermitage.*)

Hardstone tabletop with an Italian mosaic in the center. From the Winter Palace, c. 1825-1830. (*A La Vieille Russie.*)

The Great Theater (Bolshoi) in Moscow. Lithograph by Gabriel, 1799.

Brocade fur-lined coat belonging to a rich farmer's wife. North Russia, late nineteenth century. (*The Historical Museum.*)

We had another fête yesterday at the Michael Palace, home of the Grand Duchess Elena, sister-in-law of the Emperor.

The interior of the great hall was decorated with astounding richness; fifteen hundred boxes and pots of the rarest flowers formed a fragrant grove. At the end of the hall, in a copse of exotic plants, one saw a fountain of fresh clear water where a sheaflike cluster of jets spouted continuously. These jets, lighted by clusters of candles, shone like a spray of diamonds. They cooled the air, which was kept in motion by enormous palm branches and banana plants, glistening with dew, from which the breeze of the waltz shook pearls of moisture onto the moss of the balmy grove.

MARQUIS DE CUSTINE, 1839

Festival dress of a rich Cossack woman of the nineteenth century. The cream-colored satin brocade blouse has colored embroidery, and the upper sleeves are banded with gold brocade. The *sarafan* is of blue and brown brocade decorated with a re-embroidered gold lace galloon. The embroidered sash has gold tassels. (*The Hermitage.*)

Left: The Red Cabinet of the Grand Duchess Elena Pavlovna, sister of Alexander I and Nicholas I, 1885.

Court livery for a blackamoor, Winter Palace. Eight pieces: jacket, two vests, balloon trousers, fez (not shown), silk scarf, spats, soft saffron leather shoes. Second half of the nineteenth century. (*The Hermitage.*)

The Empress took her place at the horseshoe-shaped table on the dais. Behind her gilded armchair, against the marble wall, huge bunches of white and pink camellias blossomed like gigantic vegetable fireworks. Twelve tall black men, the most beautiful specimens of African races, dressed in mameluk style, with white twisted turban, green jacket with gold corners, wide red pantaloons sashed with a cachemire belt, the entire outfit braided and embroidered on every seam, walked up and down the dais steps, either giving or taking dishes from the lackeys, with those graceful and dignified movements which are peculiar to Orientals, even while they are performing servile tasks. These Orientals who had forgotten Desdemona majestically performed their duty and gave the totally European party an Asiatic flair.

THEOPHILE GAUTIER, 1865

Large floral brooch: diamonds, emeralds, gold, silver, c. 1760. (*The U.S.S.R. Diamond Fund, the Kremlin.*)

Ural Kazakh woman's festival dress, nineteenth century. The blouse is of cream satin with floral embroidery appliquéd with gold re-embroidered lace bands. The *sarafan*, of silver and beige satin brocade, has gold buttons and gold re-embroidered lace galloons. The silk sash has gold tassels. (*The Historical Museum.*)

The Emperor's carriages came to take us to the bal masqué. *130,000 people were said to be assembled. The Empress told Mr D. that upwards of four thousand carriages came to Peterhof that day, and the Emperor had four thousand horses of his own employed in the service of the Court....*

People of every class were admitted to the palace, and it was a striking spectacle to see courtly dames in gold and jewels, Emperor, Grand Dukes and Duchesses, Princes and Counts, whirling through crowds of rustics, men with long beards, women with russet gowns, who gazed with respectful astonishment, and though in close contact with these grandees, showed no symptoms of rudeness, and were as quiet and unpresuming as if they had been bred to palaces and balls. They stood close to the imperial party; there was no pushing or shoving or noise.... I should think that such a fête could only be given in Russia, where the people are so docile and orderly.

MRS. C. A. A. DISBROWE, *wife of a diplomat, 1825*

Backpiece of a woman's headdress, eighteenth century. (*The Historical Museum.*)

Left: Festival dress, late eighteenth century. The cream satin brocade *sarafan* has rose, blue, and green floral embroidery, gold buttons, and gold re-embroidered lace galloon. The long-sleeved blouse in ancient Russian form is of blue brocade with rose, blue, and cream embroidery. (*The Hermitage.*)

Festival dress, nineteenth century. The blouse is of white embroidered muslin, the overblouse of white satin floral-embroidered brocade lined in russet silk, with silver and gold re-embroidered panels. The russet silk skirt has a silver and gold band at the hem. (*The Hermitage.*)

Peasant costumes from various regions.

Tula.

Ryazan.

Orlov.

Russian folk art has its roots deep in the past of ancient Slavic tribes, as recent archaeological discoveries have revealed. Embroideries vary; in the north they sometimes include representations of birds, horses, fantastic trees, or female figures with raised arms accompanied by horsemen—subjects related to the labors of the Slavic plowman. In spring, when cattle were first put out to pasture, and in summer at mowing time, young girls came out in festive long shirts tied with a belt. On other occasions the shirt was worn under a *sarafan*.

Penza.

Voronezh.

Voronezh.

Kaluzhska.

Moscow.

141

Vologda.

Ryazan.

Folk costumes from the southern districts—Ryazan, Kaluga, Kursk, and Voronezh—are much brighter than their northern counterparts. Southern peasant women wore the *poneva*, a skirt of three lengths of checked woolen homespun, one of the most archaic garments of the eastern Slavs. On weekdays they wore a modest *poneva* trimmed with red fustian cloth. (Red is a traditional color in Russian peasant dress, signifying good. The Russian word for "red" and "beautiful" is the same— *krassnya*.) On holidays they wore a more elaborate one with multicolored embroidery. The figure of a woman wearing such a garment acquired a solemn and monumental aspect. From the birch forest, a familiar part of the Russian landscape, the women took bark to make their woven shoes (*lapti.*)

Smolensk.

Silk and velvet gloves, embroidered in gold and pearls, late eighteenth century. (*The Historical Museum.*)

Sleigh of a Russian Peasant. G. Orlovski, 1832.

Caviar vendor. G. Orlovski, 1832.

Peasant wearing a *tulup*. G. Orlovski, 1832.

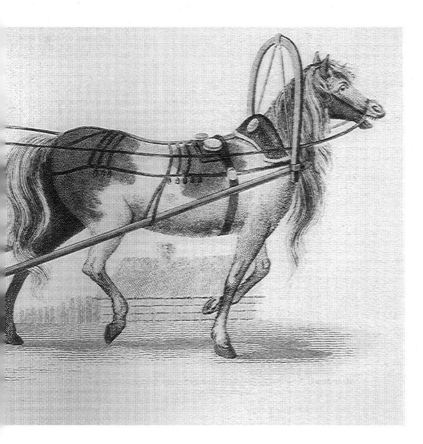

Merchant. G. Orlovski, 1832.

We arrived at the hotel where the most varied series of vehicles appeared in the large courtyard: sledges, troikas, droshkys, kibitkas, post-chaises, traveling-coaches, landaus, char-a-bancs, summer and winter coaches, for in Russia nobody walks, and if one sends a servant to buy cigars, he will take a sledge to travel the one hundred feet that separate the house from the tobacco shop.

THEOPHILE GAUTIER, 1865

The peasant who has been acquitted by the court trudges home no more elated than if he had been condemned. In either case the decision seems to him the result of capricious tyranny or chance.
　　In the same way, when he is summoned as a witness he stubbornly professes to know nothing, even in face of incontestable fact. Being found guilty by a law-court does not disgrace a man in the eyes of the Russian peasant. Exiles and convicts go by the name of unfortunates with him.

ALEXANDER HERZEN, to Jules Michelet

Overleaf: Lithograph of a military parade in a square near St. Petersburg, possibly at Tsarskoe Selo, c. 1850. (*A La Vieille Russie.*)

These simple dresses of point d'Angleterre, with their two or three flounces, cost more than a prelate's robe of gold or silver brocade; the bouquets on this skirt of tarlatan or gauze are attached with diamond knots; this velvet ribbon is clasped by a stone that could have been taken from the crown of a Tsar....

At first glance...one would think that Russian women dress with less luxury than the men. This is wrong. Like all women, they know how to render gauze more precious than gold.

THEOPHILE GAUTIER, 1865

Badge of the Order of Saint Catherine in gold, diamonds, and enamel, early nineteenth century. (*The Metropolitan Museum of Art.*)

Flounced tarlatan ball dress embroidered with flowers, with ribbon belt, 1850. (*The Hermitage.*)

Right: A lady-in-waiting in court robe and *kokochnik* with tulle veil, late nineteenth century. (*The Hermitage.*) This was the customary dress for daytime ceremonies such as weddings and baptisms, or for minor evening ceremonies such as performances in the Hermitage theater, or small court balls of only five hundred people. Pushkin called such gowns "the ladies' dress uniforms."

Miniature of Alexander II by Rokstuhl,
court miniaturist. (*A La Vieille Russie.*)

ALEXANDER II

1855-1881

Born in 1818, Alexander II was the eldest son of Nicholas I. An enlightened autocrat, Alexander was known as the Tsar Liberator for his role in freeing the serfs in 1861. He acceded to the throne during the Crimean War, which revealed the glaring backwardness of Russia in comparison with England and France, and embarked on a series of reforms designed to modernize the country. There had been six hundred miles of railway in Russia at his accession; when he died, there were fourteen thousand.

The abolition of serfdom failed to create a politically viable class, as Alexander had hoped, and it managed to undermine the foundations of Russia's already shaken landowning class. He sold Alaska to the United States in 1867, but extended Russian control of Central Asia and adopted a pan-Slavic policy that led to a victorious war against the Turks and secured the independence of Bulgaria. Various assassination attempts and the growth of nihilistic terrorist societies made him increasingly conservative in the last few years of his reign.

Spurning his wife, Maria Alexandrovna (the former Princess Marie of Hesse-Darmstadt), who had borne him six sons and two daughters, Alexander fell in love with the young Princess Catherine Dolgoruky, by whom he had three children and whom he married privately in 1880 when the Empress died. He was highly criticized for this liaison. On the day he signed a proclamation granting the zemstvos (local councils) a legislative role in the government, Alexander was assassinated by a terrorist's bomb.

During his reign and that of his son Alexander III, Russian music and literature reached great heights with the works of Turgenev, Dostoyevsky, Tolstoy, Moussorgsky, and Tchaikovsky.

Right: The Coronation of Alexander II in
the Uspensky Cathedral, Moscow, 1856.

At four o'clock I woke up to find
the promise of a glorious, warm day,
and I got up for good at five, had
breakfast at six, ate as many boiled
eggs as I possibly could..., and then
tucked myself into the carriage with
three other equally corpulent bun-
dles of silk and satin, and away
we went.... We had the best place
in the Kremlin enclosure.... The
tribune, in the second story of which
we sat, faced the Kremlin square,
which was surrounded by three
churches; the famous Red Staircase
leading to the palace, and the stands
which had been erected in all possible spaces, completed the sur-
roundings of the square.... It was a
little after seven. We got our seats in
the second row, and began to take
in the gorgeous night before us....
The square was filling with people.... The gorgeous red, white
and gold uniforms of the guards,
who lined the edges of the crimson
carpet wherever it was laid, were
quite put to shame as the many
representatives of the various orien-
tal countries began to arrive.

KATE KOON BOVEY,
Russian Coronation, 1896

Coronation ceremonies of Alexander II; saluting the people
from the Red Stair. 1856.

Family photographs of Konstantin Konstantino-
vich, nephew of Alexander II. (*A La Vieille Russie.*)

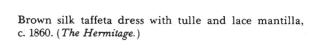

Brown silk taffeta dress with tulle and lace mantilla,
c. 1860. (*The Hermitage.*)

Alexander II and Maria Alexandrovna (at center) at a society
ball in the 1850s, St. Petersburg.

*In Russia, court balls open with a polonaise; it is not a dance,
but a sort of parade, a march with torches which has great
character. The participants form two lines, leaving an aisle
down the middle of the ballroom.... The orchestra plays an
air, majestic and slow, and the promenade begins, led by the
Emperor, who gives his hand to a princess or to a lady whom
he wishes to honor.*

*The Emperor Alexander II that evening wore an ele-
gant military uniform which showed off his slender waist; a
white jacket reaching to mid-thigh, with gold brandenbourgs,
bordered with blue Siberian fox at the neck, wrists, and hem,
starred on the breast with his many decorations. His tight sky-
blue trousers tapered down to his narrow boots.*

*Following the Imperial Family were the high officers
of the Palace and of the Court, each giving his hand to a
lady.... Occasionally a young Circassian prince, a Lesghin
chieftain, a Mongol officer join the cortege.... What is more
natural than to see a Mohammedan prince dancing the polonaise with a Greek-Orthodox noblewoman of St. Petersburg?
Are they not both subjects of the Emperor of all the Russias?*

THEOPHILE GAUTIER, 1865

White broadcloth burnoose with tasseled hood, embroidered with garlands, 1860. (*The Hermitage.*)

Overleaf: Fanny Elssler dancing "La Esmerelda" in St.
Petersburg, 1848. (*Bakushnin Theater Museum, Moscow.
Novosti.*)

Vignettes of a court ball at the Winter Palace, 1859. Center, foreground: Tsar Alexander II. At left, just above the lowest range of figures, is the Tsarevich, leading his partner to the dance. The drawings show personalities of the time, in Winter Palace settings.

Princess Yussupova's batiste morning dress with crinoline, embroidered all over with satin stitch, c. 1860. (*The Hermitage.*)

Below: Woven cloth-of-silver court dress. By Mme. Olga (O. N. Bulbenkova), St. Petersburg. (*The Hermitage.*) (See pages 18-19.)

The Great Chapel in the Winter Palace. Drawing by Sadovnikov.

Right: A lady of St. Petersburg, in a three-piece gown with bustle, c. 1870. (*The Hermitage.*) Such dresses with a surfeit of decoration fitted harmoniously into the salons of the period, rooms overloaded with furniture, gilt, upholstery, massive draperies, and elaborate picture frames.

Photographs of the Russian bourgeoisie. Karetin, c. 1870.

Overleaf: Blindman's bluff. Karetin, c. 1870.

ALEXANDER III

1881-1894

A man of limited intelligence and education, Alexander III, born in 1845, was known for his reactionary policies, to which the assassination of his father and the influence of conservative advisers had contributed. He increased the repressive power of the police, tightened censorship, limited the power of the zemstvos (local councils) and the judiciary, increased controls over the peasantry, subjected national minorities to russification, and persecuted all religious minorities, especially the Jews. But industrialization increased during his reign, which saw the beginning of the Trans-Siberian Railroad, and he strove for peace in Europe, while gradually extending Russian domination in Central Asia.

In the arts, the golden age of the realistic novel was over, replaced by Chekhovian despair at "the period of small deeds." Borodin composed *Prince Igor.* The ballets and operas of Tchaikovsky provided interludes of fantasy for a harassed people; *Eugene Onegin* was Alexander's favorite opera.

Parsimonious and not particularly fond of ceremony, Alexander did not move to the Winter Palace but continued to live at the Anichkov Palace after his accession. He was married to Princess Dagmar of Denmark, Maria Feodorovna, and was succeeded by their son Nicholas II.

Above: Alexander III.

Presentation gold snuffbox with crowned diamond monogram of Alexander III. Fried and Kochli, St. Petersburg. (*A La Vieille Russie.*)

Vorontsov Palace, by Bartolomeo Rastrelli. It was used in the eighteenth century as the training school for court pages. Pages from aristocratic families were assured of rising, after graduation, to top posts in the army, administration, and diplomacy—fields closed to those of lower birth. Drawing by Joseph Charlemagne.

Court uniform of a senator, second half of the nineteenth century. Red coat with gold embroidery of oak leaves and laurel. White trousers with gold braid. Blue ribbon of the Order of Saint Andrew. Saber. (*The Hermitage.*) (See page 18.)

Left: Court uniform of a gentleman-in-waiting. Black broadcloth coat with gold embroidery, white trousers with gold stripe. Blue ribbon of the Order of Saint Vladimir, with key attached. Saber. (Not shown: black felt hat with gold embroidery and white plumes.)

The streets became more animated;...more and more rarely did he encounter jehus with latticed wooden sleighs, studded over with gilt nails—on the contrary, he kept coming across first-class drivers in caps of raspberry-hued velvet, their sleighs lacquered and with bearskin robes, while the carriages had decorated seats for the drivers and raced down the roadway, their wheels screeching over the snow.

NIKOLAI GOGOL, "The Overcoat"

Hardstone porphyry figure of a first-class driver. Fabergé. (*A La Vieille Russie.*)

Balalaika. (*The Metropolitan Museum of Art.*)

Right: Russian peasants drinking and playing the balalaika.

Woman's boots, early twentieth century. (*The Historical Museum.*)

The boots alone were a whole poem of wretchedness and decay.

THEOPHILE GAUTIER, 1865

A rich girl from Kirghiz, 1836. Solntzev, 1869.

One went to the gypsies. They lived in small houses on the outskirts, on the islands of St. Petersburg. One used to go there at night in a troika, after dining at a restaurant. The room would be very simple, with whitewashed walls, maybe one beautiful chandelier, a comfortable chair, and lots of champagne and fruit. You ordered, and baskets of champagne were brought in.

And they sang and they danced. How they sang! The Russian mind is monotonous, tremendous gaiety or tremendous despair, no middle. They would sing of death and of suicide and of going away from the world into a monastery if a girl refused to marry.

Then at early morning we would return from there...wild parties, strange, I can still see it.

COUNT VASSILY ADLERBERG, great-grandson of the High Chamberlain at the Court of Nicholas I; grandson of the High Chamberlain at the Court of Alexander II; son of the Governer General of St. Petersburg

Gypsies dancing, 1830. Solntzev, 1869.

Portrait of Olga Orlova. Valentin Serov, 1911. (*The Russian Museum.*)

A lady of St. Petersburg wearing an at-home costume of satin appliquéd with lace. (*The Hermitage.*)

Evening dress with swansdown stole. N. Lamanova, 1940. (*The Hermitage.*) Lamanova opened an atelier in 1885 in Moscow. After World War I she continued to make costumes, among them those for the film *Alexander Nevsky*.

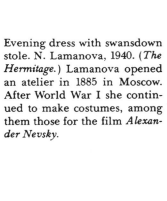

Evening dress with bead embroidery and fur trim. Paul Poiret, c. 1910. (*The Hermitage.*) Poiret was inspired by the costumes and sets of Bakst and Benois when Diaghilev first brought the Ballet Russe to Paris in 1909.

Evening dress, two-piece, black satin with jet embroidery. Worth, 1890. (*The Hermitage.*)

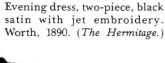

The White Vestibule and Staircase, designed by I. A. Monighetti in 1860 for Maria Alexandrovna, wife of Alexander II, at Tsarskoe Selo.

Gilded silver samovar of the Tsarevich Alexander Alexandrovich (Alexander III). Nichols and Plinke (Magasin Anglais), St. Petersburg, 1866. (*A La Vieille Russie.*)

We all arrived separately at the door of the Palace where Prince Galitzine, Vice Chamberlain, and another Vice received us in evening dress and stars.

Their apartment was magnificent. A drawing room "blue satin", bedroom "red satin".... Almost everything is new and smart, but whatever is not new is dusty.

Lady Emma who is...sensitive..., declares that she has a Mujik in her apartment, she first thought concealed a spy, now she thinks a deceased one and that no efforts of hers to purify it are of any avail. Oh! the smells—natural and artificial—are past all belief.

LADY AUGUSTA STANLEY, 1874

Costumes of the sixteenth and seventeenth centuries, re-created for a ball at the Winter Palace in February 1903. From left to right: A noblewoman dressed as a boyarina. (*The Hermitage.*) Three photos from an album commemorating the ball: "His Imperial Highness, Monseigneur, the Grand Duke Alexis Alexandrovich as a boyar at the Court of Tsar Alexei Mikhailovich (father of Peter I)."

"Her Imperial Highness, Madame the Grand Duchess Marie Gueorguievna, as a seventeenth-century townswoman from Torjok." "His Imperial Highness, Monseigneur, the Grand Duke Mikhail Alexandrovich as a seventeenth-century Tsarevich dressed for a military review."

BIBLIOGRAPHY

Ascher, Abraham, and the Editors of Newsweek Book Division, *The Kremlin*. (New York: Newsweek, 1972.)

Benois, Alexandre, editor, *Les Tresors d'Art en Russie* (periodical), six volumes. (St. Petersburg, 1901-1906.)

Billington, James H., *The Icon and the Axe: An Interpretative History of Russian Culture*. (London: Weidenfeld and Nicholson, and New York: Knopf, 1966.)

Carmichael, Joel. *An Illustrated History of Russia*. (New York: Reynal, n.d.)

Catherine II, *Memoirs*. Translated and with notes by Katharine Anthony. (London and New York: Knopf, 1927.)

Catherine II, *Memoirs*. Edited by Dominique Maroger, translated by Moura Budberg. (London: Hamish Hamilton, 1955, and New York: Macmillan, 1961.)

Coughlan, Robert, *Elizabeth and Catherine, Empresses of All the Russias*. (New York: Putnam, 1974, and London: MacDonald and Jane's, 1975.)

Coxe, William, *Travels into Poland, Russia, Sweden and Denmark*. (London, 1784.) *Travels in Poland and Russia* (New York: Arno, 1970.)

Crankshaw, Edward, *The Shadow of the Winter Palace*. (London: Macmillan, and New York: Viking, 1976.)

Crankshaw, Edward, *Tolstoy: The Making of a Novelist*. (London: Weidenfeld and Nicholson, and New York: Viking, 1974.)

Custine, Marquise de, *Lettres de Russie: La Russie en 1839*. (Paris: Gallimard, 1975.) *Custine's Eternal Russia*. Edited and translated by Phyllis Penn Kohler. (Coral Gables, Florida: University of Miami, 1976.)

Dimsdale, Elizabeth. From an unpublished diary of 1781, quoted in Kennett, and used by gracious permission of Baron Dimsdale.

Disbrowe, C. A. A., *Original Letters from Russia, 1825-28*. (London, 1878.)

Dumas, Alexandre, *Adventures in Czarist Russia*. Translated and edited by A. E. Murch. (London: Peter Owen, and Philadelphia: Chilton, 1961.)

The Englishwoman in Russia. (London, 1855.)

Gautier, Theophile, *Voyage en Russie*. (Paris: Hachette, 1961.)

Graham, Stephen, *Peter the Great*. (London: Ernest Benn, and New York: Simon and Schuster, 1929.)

Grimm, Baron Friedrich Melchior von, *Correspondance Artistique avec Catherine II*. (Paris, 1932.)

Guerney, Bernard Guilbert, ed., *The Portable Russian Reader*. (New York: Viking, 1947.)

Hamilton, George Heard, *The Art and Architecture of Russia*. (Harmondsworth and Baltimore: Penguin, 1954.)

Hingley, Ronald, *A Concise History of Russia*. (London: Thames and Hudson, and New York: Viking, 1972.)

The Horizon Book of the Arts of Russia (New York: Horizon, 1970.)

Hürlimann, Martin, *Moscow and Leningrad*. (London: Thames and Hudson, and New York: Viking, 1958.)

Kennett, Audrey and Victor, *The Palaces of Leningrad*. (London: Thames and Hudson, and New York: Putnam, 1973.)

Kluchevsky, V. O., *A History of Russia*. Translated by C. J. Hogarth. (London: Dent, and New York: Dutton, 1926.)

Korb, Johann Georg. *Scenes from the Court of Peter the Great*. Edited by F. L. Glaser. (New York: N. L. Broan, 1921.)

Kuchumov, A. M., *Pavlovsk*. (Leningrad, 1970.)

Letters from a Lady Who Resided Some Years in Russia, to Her Friend in England. (London: Dodsley, 1775.)

Loukomski, G. K., *Mobilier et Décoration des Anciens Palais Imperiaux Russes*. (Paris, 1928.)

Loukomski, G. K., *La Vie et les Moeurs en Russie de Pierre le Grand à Lénine*. (Paris, 1928.)

Oldenbourg, Zoé, *Catherine the Great*. Translated from the French by Anne Carter. (London: Heinemann, and New York: Pantheon, 1965.)

Olearius, Adam, *Voyages*. (1656.)

Paul of Aleppo, *The Travels of Macarius, Patriarch of Antioch*. (London, 1836.)

Pushkin, Alexander, *Eugene Onegin, A Novel in Verse*, translated from the Russian with a commentary by Vladimir Nabokov. (London: Routledge and Kegan Paul, and Princeton, N.J.: Princeton University Press, Bollingen Series LXII, 1964; revised edition, 1974.)

Pushkin, Alexander, *Poems, Prose and Plays*. Edited by Avrahm Yarmolinsky. (New York: Modern Library, 1936. *Queen of Spades* translated by T. Keane.)

Shoberl, Frederic, *The World in Miniature—Russia*. (London, 1823.)

Stanley, Lady Augusta, *Later Letters*. Edited by the Dean of Windsor and Hector Bolitho. (New York and London: Jonathan Cape, 1929.)

Swinton, Andrew, *Travels into Norway, Denmark and Russia in the Years 1788-1791*. (London, 1792.)

Tolstoy, Leo, *Anna Karenin*. Translated by Rosemary Edmonds. London and New York: Penguin.)

Tolstoy, Leo, *War and Peace*. Translated by Louise and Aylmer Maude. (London: Oxford University Press, and New York: Simon and Schuster, 1942.)

PHOTO CREDITS

The editors and the publishers wish to thank the following for their kind permission to reproduce the photographs which appear on the pages noted:

A La Vieille Russie: pages 12 l, 80 tr, 85, 116 b, 176 l.

The Bettman Archive: page 171.

Candace Fischer: pages 1, 2, 3, 4, 12 t, 12 b, 30-31 t, 34-35 b, 35 r, 42 l, 42 bc, 44 tl, 45 c, 45 br, 46 bl, 47 tr, 47 bl, 52 t, 67 t, 68 l, 68-69, 69, 94, 96-97, 104 t, 104-105 b, 108 cl, 109, 112 l, 112-113 t, 112-113 c, 112-113 b, 113 r, 130 tl, 130 bl, 131 tr, 131 br, 172, 173.

John R. Freeman and Co. (European Collection): pages 153, 157.

Helga Studio: pages 33 tl, 62 tr, 79 l, 88, 110, 118 c, 126 cl, 126-127 t, 126-127 b, 135 bl, 148-149, 152, 156 cr, 168 b, 170 tr.

The Hermitage Museum: pages 30 b, 31 b, 32 l, 32 r, 33 bl, 33 r, 36 l, 37 r, 38 l, 56, 57 r, 62 l, 63 r, 64 l, 65 r, 70 tl, 90 l, 91 br, 95 tl, 116 cl, 117 t, 120 l, 121 r, 122 l, 122 br, 134 bl, 136 l, 136 br, 137, 138 br, 139, 150 l, 151, 156 bl, 157 br, 160 l, 161, 163, 169 bl, 169 cr, 174-175 t, 174-175 b, 175 tr, 175 b, 178 l, 178 r, 179 l, 179 r.

Victor Kennett: pages 31 r, 46 tl, 60, 62 br, 64-65 c, 70 rc, 71, 75, 78 tr, 82, 84, 87, 89, 90-91, 92-93, 98 t, 99, 116-117, 117 br, 120-121, 128-129, 160-161, 162, 168-169 t.

The Kremlin Museum: pages 38-39 t, 38-39 b, 40 tl, 40 bc, 41 r.

The Metropolitan Museum of Art Photographic Services—

William Pons, Photographer: pages 11, 13 t, 29, 30 l, 34 l, 36-37 t, 36-37 b, 38 cr, 39, 42-43, 48-49, 50, 51, 52 b, 54-55, 56-57, 58, 61, 63 t, 66, 67 t, 72-73 c, 74 t, 74 l, 74 br, 76 tl, 76 br, 76-77, 77 r, 78 br, 79 tr, 79 br, 83, 86, 90 br, 95 cr, 98 b, 102 t, 102 b, 103 b, 104 b, 105 r, 106 bl, 106-107 t, 107 r, 108 tr, 115 t, 115 c, 118 t, 118 b, 119, 122-123 t, 123 br, 124, 125, 134-135 t, 136-137, 146 l, 146 br, 146-147 t, 147, 150 t, 168 tl, 170 c.

Inge Morath: pages 7, 13 r, 53, 81, 176-177, 180.

Novosti: pages 158-159.

The New York Public Library, Astor, Lenox and Tilden Foundations: pages 40 tc, 43 r, 154-155, 164, 165, 166-167.

The State Historical Museum, Moscow: pages 72 l, 73 r, 80 l, 127 r, 130 tr, 131 bl, 132 cl, 132 tr, 132 br, 133, 135 r, 138 tl, 138 tr, 140 l, 140 tr, 140 cr, 140 b, 141 tl, 141 cl, 141 bl, 141 r, 142 l, 142 c, 143, 144-145, 170 br.

Thames and Hudson: pages 28, 34-35 t, 59, 100-101.

Malcolm Varon: pages 17-24.

Sources unidentified: pages 111 and 114, from *An Illustrated History of Russia*, by Joel Carmichael (New York: Reynal and Co.); page 174, from *L'Art Russe — Oeuvres Choisies* (Leningrad: Editions d'Art Aurore).